EDEXCEL

A LEVEL
MUSIC

Revision
Guide

ALISTAIR WIGHTMAN

RHINEGOLD
EDUCATION

First published 2017 in Great Britain by
Rhinegold Education
14-15 Berners Street
London W1T 3LJ, UK
www.rhinegoldeducation.co.uk

© 2017 Rhinegold Education
a division of Music Sales Limited

> You should always check the current
> requirements of your examination,
> since these may change.

Editor: Katharine Allenby
Cover and book design: Fresh Lemon Australia

Edexcel A Level Music Revision Guide
Order No. RHG344
ISBN: 978-1-78558-172-4

Exclusive Distributors:
Music Sales Ltd
Distribution Centre, Newmarket Road
Bury St Edmunds, Suffolk IP33 3YB, UK

Printed in the EU

Contents

THE AUTHOR

The author

Alistair Wightman

has worked in primary, secondary and further education, and
is now a freelance teacher and writer. For many years he was
a principal examiner in history and analysis in A Level music.

His publications include *Writing about Music* (Rhinegold, 2008)
and several books and articles on Polish music, including *Karlowicz,
Young Poland and the Musical Fin-de-siecle* (Ashgate, 1996),
Karol Szymanowski: his Life and Music (Ashgate, 1999),
Szymanowski on Music: Selected Writings of Karol Szymanowski
(Toccata Press, 1999), and *Szymanowski's King Roger, the opera
and its origins* (Toccata Press, 2015).

Edexcel A Level Music (Code 9MU0) has three components:

1. **Performing**	Recorded recital	**60 marks:** 30% of the total A Level mark
2. **Composing**	Two compositions	**60 marks:** 30% of the total A Level mark
3. **Appraising**	Written examination	**100 marks:** 40% of the total A Level mark

This guide will help you revise for **Component 3,** an externally assessed examination that lasts two hours. Some guidance is given here on tackling **Section A** questions (Areas of Study and Dictation), but the main focus will be on **Section B** (Extended Response), which requires you to answer a question about various musical features of the set works.

Pages 12-17 contain an overview of the terminology that will be used in the Section B (essay 2) questions, along with a list of the features you would be expected to mention in your answers.

On pages 18-143 are revision notes for each of the set works, giving a brief historical context, followed by pointers to the most important technical features of the music:

- Rhythm and metre
- Melody
- Harmony
- Tonality
- Texture
- Performance resources
- Music notation
- Structure.

The final sections of the book comprise sample essay questions and responses, followed by a glossary.

For practice materials for Sections A and B (essay 1), i.e. the listening questions, consult Rhinegold Education's *Edexcel AS/A level Music Listening Tests 2016*.

The marks for **Component 3** total 100, with the following breakdown:

Section A	Listening (Relating to Areas of Study and Dictation)	**50 marks**
Section B	Essay 1 (Relating an unfamiliar extract to set works)	**20 marks**
Section B	Essay 2	**30 marks**

At the start of the summer term, it is quite likely that you will still be finishing Components 1 and 2. It is in your interest to complete these assignments as soon as you can, in order to maximise the time available for preparing for the Unit 3 examination.

Set works

With the exception of the dictation test, the whole of the Component 3 written examination revolves around the **prescribed works** in the *Edexcel AS/A level Anthology of Music*. You are required to study **all** the works within the six Areas of Study listed below.

Section A consists of three listening tests with skeleton scores and recordings, which cover the set works (in addition to the dictation text).

For **Section B (essay 1)**, you have to listen to an extract of unfamiliar music, which you then relate to appropriate set works.

For **Section B (essay 2)**, you answer one of three questions on set works. No recordings are available for this question, but you will have a resource booklet that contains a printed extract, if not the whole of the work. Consequently, you will be expected to depend on your knowledge of the work as a whole, as you may not have the complete score to hand.

The set works for A Level are divided into six genres:

Vocal music

- Cantata 'Ein feste Burg ist unser Gott' BWV 80, 1st, 2nd and 8th movements (Bach)

- *Die Zauberflöte*, excerpts from Act I: No. 4 'Queen of the Night' and No. 5 'Quintet' (Mozart)

- *On Wenlock Edge,* No. 1 'On Wenlock Edge', No. 3 'Is My Team Ploughing?' and No. 5 'Bredon Hill' (Vaughan Williams)

Instrumental music

- Concerto in D minor Op. 3 No. 11 RV 565 (Vivaldi)

- Piano Trio in G minor Op. 17, 1st movement (Clara Schumann)

- *Symphonie fantastique*, 1st movement (Berlioz)

Music for film

- Cues from *The Duchess* (2008): 'The Duchess' (Opening and End titles), 'Mistake of your life', 'Six years later' and 'Never see your children again' (Rachel Portman)

- Cues from *Batman Returns* (1992): Main theme ('Birth of a Penguin Part II'), 'Birth of a Penguin Part I', 'Batman vs the Circus' and 'The Rise and Fall from Grace' (Danny Elfman)

- Cues from *Psycho* (1960): 'Prelude', 'The City', 'Marion', 'The Murder', 'The Toys', 'The Cellar', 'Discovery' and 'Finale' (Bernard Herrmann)

Popular music and jazz

- Tracks from *Back in the Day*: 'Lady Day and (John Coltrane)', 'Inner State (of Mind)' and 'Love and affection' (Courtney Pine)

- Tracks from *Hounds of Love*: 'Cloudbusting', 'And Dream of Sheep' and 'Under Ice' (Kate Bush)

- Tracks from *Revolver:* 'Eleanor Rigby', 'Here, There and Everywhere', 'I Want to Tell You' and 'Tomorrow Never Knows' (The Beatles)

Fusions

- *Estampes*, Nos. 1 and 2 ('Pagodes' and 'La Soirée dans Grenade') (Debussy)

- Tracks from *Caña Quema*: 'Allá va candela' and 'Se quema la chumbambá' (La Familia Valera Miranda)

- Tracks from *Breathing Under Water:* 'Burn', 'Breathing Under Water' and 'Easy' (Anoushka Shankar)

New directions

- Three Dances for Two Prepared Pianos, No. 1 (John Cage)

- *Petals* (Kaija Saariaho)

- *Le sacre du printemps (The Rite of Spring):* Introduction, 'Les augures printaniers' and 'Jeu du rapt' (Stravinsky)

Section A: Listening

In the exam you can listen to a short extract from the selected set works as many times as you wish. (Take care to manage the time available to your best advantage.) You will be provided with a single-line skeleton score of the extract, showing locations of the features you have to describe.

You will have to demonstrate your analytical knowledge and aural skills by identifying aspects such as:

- Instruments and/or voices
- Textures
- Rhythmic devices and patterns
- Melodic aspects
- Features of word-setting
- Keys, cadences and chords
- Harmonic devices
- Structure of the extract
- Location of the extract within the work.

By the time you take the exam, you should be totally familiar with the music, and be able to rely on analytical information you have already absorbed. Remember, though, that the extract's bar numbering may not correspond with the numbering in the Anthology.

Top tips

You should practise for the Section A exam as often as you can. Make sure you get in the habit of:

- Seeing how many marks are available for each question (and therefore how much information is required)
- Working out plausible possibilities (such as related keys) to support your impressions
- Using correct terms (keep referring to the terminology chapter on pages 12-17 of this book) to avoid long-winded explanations
- Using strategies in dictation tests to enable you to maximise your mark, such as:
  - First noting the number of sounds you hear by jotting down a dot for each note
  - Working out where the bar lines fall, and then establishing individual note lengths
  - Charting pitches, being mindful of surrounding melody notes in the given parts.

Useful resources are the Sample Assessment Materials provided by Edexcel (ISBN 978-1-4469-3192-9) and Rhinegold Education's *Edexcel AS/A Level Music Listening Tests* 2016 (RHG 342).

Section B: Extended responses

In this section you answer **two** questions. The first of these is a listening test, which requires you to respond to a piece of unfamiliar music. The information in the chapters that follow will help you become familiar with the terminology required to answer the first question, and also apply it to the second question based on the set works.

This guide will help you to:

- Revise the key facts for each set work
- Practise writing essay answers that incorporate these key facts
- Improve the way you express your ideas.

Top tips

Keep listening to your prescribed works so that you begin to recognise and locate the key features covered in this guide. Remember also that, besides being able to analyse various musical works, you need to be able to present your arguments as clearly as possible; you may have to compare, contrast, assess, evaluate and comment as necessary.

Time management is a vital aspect of any exam. You are issued with a CD and can listen to the tests as many times as you like. This approach is intended to be helpful to you, but you must take care not to spend excessive amounts of time on one question at the expense of others. You should experiment with trial materials in order to find the optimum time you can allow for each question.

Perhaps as a starting-point, you may find it helpful to allow approximately:

- Ten minutes for each Section A listening test
- A further ten minutes for the dictation questions
- This will leave you with one hour and 20 minutes, which you could then divide into 30 minutes for essay 1 in Section B and 50 minutes for essay 2 in Section B.

Consider the following points:

- Take care not to stray from the question, because you may be penalised for irrelevance. (If the question asks for information about 'harmony', you won't get any marks for writing about melody)
- Keep referring to the terminology section, to be sure that you are focusing on the correct features of the music
- Do not worry if, sometimes, you seem to be stating the obvious! That is what examiners expect to see
- You don't need to include musical examples to gain full marks, and because you don't take a copy of the Anthology into the exam, you won't be expected

to mention specific bar numbers. (However, try to be as precise as possible when describing specific sections of the music.)

- Keep listening to your set works, and following them in the Anthology
- You should write in continuous prose for both essays in Section B. If you begin to run out of time, however, use bullet points to ensure that everything you wish to say is included.

In addition to revision schemes, the final chapter of this guide provides examples of questions, indicative content (mark schemes) and specimen answers with commentaries for you to study.

FURTHER READING

- *Dictionary of Music in Sound* by David Bowman (ISBN 978-0-946890-87-3, RHG500)
- *Writing about Music Workbook* by Alistair Wightman (ISBN 978-1-906178-38-3, RHG429)
- *Edexcel AS/A Level Music Study Guide 2016* by Hugh Benham and Alistair Wightman (ISBN 978-1-78558-169-4, RHG341)

Revision notes

Pages 18-143 provide a series of points that should help you to focus on the most important aspects of each set work. The 18 set works covered in this guide are divided into six sections corresponding to the areas of study.

Edexcel has issued some guidance on how best to approach these examinations in a series of responses to frequently asked questions. They state at one point that students are expected to be 'familiar with the set works but are not expected to know each piece in depth'. But in response to a question about whether students need to reference bar and beats of the set works, they say that 'students should be aware of and be able to make reference to (where the question demands) the bar and beats of the set works in the Appraising exam'.

We suggest you try to develop an overview of each piece by checking that you understand the main points, using the terminology covered in the following chapter. After this, try to absorb some of the additional points, which will lead you to draw up examples that can be used to illustrate the work in question.

It is most important that you keep referring to the Anthology, and associate the points made in the lists that follow with what you hear in the music and read in the score. An attempt to learn these points in the form of abstract crib notes means you do not get anything out of the exercise long term, and run the risk of error.

Terminology

This section includes many of the terms you will need to know for your exam, but it is not exhaustive. You may not need to comment on all the points listed below for each and every set work.

In this guide, beats of the bar appear in superscipt when part of a bar reference. For example, 'bar 4^3' means 'bar four, beat three'.

Rhythm and metre

When writing about rhythm and metre, comment on:

- The variety of note lengths
- Recurring rhythmic patterns
- Dotted rhythms, or the 'reversed' dotted rhythm described as either a Scotch snap or Lombardic rhythm
- Syncopation
- Hemiola
- Triplets or other tuplets
- The time signature – whether it is simple or compound, duple, triple, quadruple or quintuple
- Metre changes
- Whether there is a metre at all.

Melody

When writing about melody, comment on:

- The range of the melody
- Whether it is in a major or minor key, or else modal or atonal
- Whether it is diatonic or chromatic
- The phrase structure – whether it is made up of balanced phrases ('periodic' phrasing) or something less regular
- Use of repetition or sequence
- Whether the melody is monotone (single note), conjunct (moving by step) or disjunct (moving by leap). If moving by leap, be ready to describe some of the intervals

- Use of motifs
- Whether the melody line is flowing or broken up by rests.

If you are describing vocal music, you will also be able to comment on aspects of text-setting:

- Whether the setting is syllabic (one note per syllable) or melismatic (several notes to a syllable)
- Whether verbal and musical accents coincide – in other words, whether the stressed syllables fall on the first beat or other strong beats of the bar, or not.

Harmony

You will be commenting on the music's vertical structure – the chords – and how they proceed from one to another. You may have to consider whether the chord is:

- A primary or secondary triad
- An augmented or diminished triad
- In root position or inverted
- Diatonic or chromatic
- Functional (broadly speaking, with cadential harmony that defines the key) or whether unrelated chords are used.

Other harmonic devices you may have to describe include:

- Cadences (perfect, imperfect/phrygian, plagal, interrupted)
- Tonic or dominant pedals (specify which, and mention if the pedal is inverted)
- Circle of 5ths
- Tierce de Picardie.

You should also be prepared to comment on the presence of particular types of dissonance:

- Suspension
- False relation
- Appoggiatura
- 7th chords, or one of the higher dissonances (9th, 11th, 13th) – and also whether they are resolved
- Added 6th, augmented 6th, diminished 7th, Neapolitan 6th
- Added-note chords.

Tonality

Tonality is not another word for sound quality or timbre. It is about whether the music has a key, and you will have to be ready to consider the following points:

- Is the music tonal or atonal?
- If the music is tonal, is the harmony functional (with cadences that define the key)?
- Is the harmony non-functional? Perhaps the music still has a key signature, but is better regarded as being 'on' rather than 'in' the key?
- Some pieces might be modal – in which case, name the mode and the key it is based on. (Be careful: the music may not be modal throughout, or else may change modes as it goes on.)

> Remember that in tonality questions, you may have to associate a theme with its key to establish a location. Such references replace the use of bar numbers which would not be expected as you do not have access to the Anthology in the exam.

- In popular music, there are frequent pentatonic elements, and in these cases it is important to name the key as well – for example, E pentatonic major.
- Does the music modulate (change key systematically), as in most classical works, or does it abruptly 'shift' from one tonal centre to another?

Texture

This term applies to the way instruments/voices are combined to sound together, and also the number of parts involved. The number of parts will affect the density of the sound.

> It is not enough at this level to describe a texture as 'thick' or 'thin'. You should aim, wherever possible, to state the number of parts, as well as the type of texture involved.

Types of texture include:

Monophonic	A single (unaccompanied) melody. (Note that a melody with a drone accompaniment is regarded as monophonic.)
Polyphonic	This term tends to be used as another way of saying contrapuntal – the combination of independently moving melody lines. It is generally better to reserve its use for early music, especially choral music of the Renaissance era.
Contrapuntal	See above. This term is freely applied in discussions of music from any period. The combination of independently moving lines may be: ▪ Free: when there is no melodic similarity between the parts ▪ Imitative: when another part enters with the same theme, while the first continues with its own music ▪ Canonic: a strict form of imitation, when the second part is near enough an exact copy of the first, even if at a different pitch ▪ Fugal: as in a fugue or fugato.

Do not confuse 'imitation' with repetition, antiphony or call-and-response.

If the passage is canonic, say whether the canon is at the octave, at the unison (the same pitch), at the 4th below, and so on. State, also, the length between the imitation – for example, two beats, one bar.

Make sure you can apply fugal terms, such as subject, answer, counter-subject, stretto, middle entry, codetta and so on.

Homophony	▪ Chordal textures, sometimes also described as homorhythmic: all parts having the same rhythm. ▪ Melody-dominated homophony: textures in which the melody is supported by a rhythmically independent part – for example, Alberti bass or broken-chord patterns. You may prefer to use the expression 'melody and accompaniment'.

Where the movement could be described as being in melody-dominated homophony, don't forget to mention transfers of the melody (for example from treble to bass), changes in accompanying patterns, and the numbers of parts (the density) used at any one time.

Heterophony	When a melody line is heard along with a rhythmically different or melodically varied version of itself.
Antiphony	When passages of music are performed by different singers and/or instrumentalists in alternation. The groups do not have to be evenly balanced. 'Call-and-response' also refers to antiphony, particularly in jazz and popular music.

Other textural features include:

- Octaves – don't forget to say how many octaves there are, or to differentiate between octaves and unison
- Pedal points – also regarded as harmonic and tonal devices, although they have some bearing on the make-up of texture as well
- Ostinato – a short repeated melodic and/or rhythmic figure, heard in conjunction with other musical ideas. It also plays a prominent role in the overall texture
- Riff – a term for ostinato used in connection with jazz and popular music.

Performance forces and timbre

'Performance forces' simply means the voices and instruments used. You may also have to discuss methods of notation.

Timbre refers to the nature of the sound produced. Be ready to comment on the use of particular ranges (tessitura) of instruments or voices, as this may contribute to the overall sound created. For example, generally low sounds may be used to produce melancholy effects.

Also be ready to describe the effects of plucking and bowing, use of mutes, harmonics, and different bowing techniques, such as *sul ponticello*, *sul tasto*, or *sur la touche*.

Structure

Many questions will require you to comment on the structure or form of a given work. The most frequently encountered structural terms are as follows:

- Binary
- Rounded binary
- Ternary
- Fugue
- Sonata form

- Rondo
- Sonata rondo
- Variations
- Ritornello
- Through-composed

- Strophic
- Ground bass
- 12-bar blues
- Verse and refrain
- Tripartite.

Once you have identified the structure in general terms, be ready to give a more detailed description of the main sections in the music, giving changes of key and specific descriptive terms (e.g. first subject, exposition and so on).

Having identified the structure, avoid falling back on 'abstract' descriptions of the music. This can be a particular temptation in sonata form movements, but it is no use telling the examiner that there is an exposition with a first subject, transition and second subject without giving some information about keys and locations.

Historical context

You should be aware of the circumstances of composition and performance for each set work. It is also important to know how music from different eras, cultural and social backgrounds has developed with the passing of time.

With that in mind, you should collect information on the date and place of the first performance (where possible), and be clear who might have commissioned the music in the first place, the purpose of the music and the nature of the original audience. For example, if writing about sacred music, be ready to comment on the type of church and service, and when writing about jazz or popular music, bear in mind differences between live and studio performance.

AREA OF STUDY 1:
Vocal music

Cantata 'Ein feste Burg ist unser Gott' BWV 80, 1st, 2nd and 8th movements (Bach)

Context

- A late-Baroque work, first performed on 31 October 1730 at St Thomas' Church in Leipzig where Bach was musical director. It was composed to mark the Festival of the Reformation – the celebration of Martin Luther's break with the Roman Catholic Church
- The Lutheran Cantata was performed before the sermon and reflected the subject of the day conveyed in the preceding reading (in this case Revelation 14, vs. 6–8)
- This type of cantata required vocal soloists, a small chorus, orchestra and continuo
- The full cantata is a multi-movement work, which – besides chorus, recitatives, arias and duets – includes a chorale for congregational use
- The text (in German) is taken from Martin Luther's hymn (known in English as 'A Stronghold Sure') for movements 1, 2, 5 and 8, and the remaining movements are settings of texts by Salomo Franck
- In the second movement, the chorale tune and text (soprano) are heard alongside Franck's poetry (bass).

Instrumental forces

- **Movement 1** is scored for four-part chorus (SATB), three oboes including: a taille (akin to cor anglais); strings consisting of violins I and II, viola, cello and violone (similar in range to double bass); and continuo instruments (organ and cembalo (harpsichord))
- Violins and viola double the soprano, alto and tenor lines, but the cello 'shadows' the bass, sometimes elaborating in heterophony
- **Movement 2** is a vocal duet for soprano and bass; the soprano doubled by oboe, sometimes in heterophony
- Violins I, II and violas provide an obbligato line in unison (a prominent and essential independent melody), supported by continuo

- **Movement 8**, the chorale, requires SATB with each part doubled by instruments: soprano and alto by oboe d'amore and violins; tenor by taille and viola; bass by continuo instruments.

Notation

- Various forms of traditional stave notation are employed
- Movement 1 has one stave for each instrument and vocal part, with cello and cembalo sharing a stave, and violone and organ allotted another
- In movement 2, violins and violas are combined on the one stave
- The chorale in movement 8 is laid out in open score, with indications regarding instrumentation at the start
- No dynamics are given, as is usual in Baroque music
- Harmonic content is indicated by figured bass, a form of musical shorthand in which each number below the bass line refers to an interval above.

For further information on figured bass and the various symbols used, see *A2 Harmony Workbook* (Rhinegold Education, 2009) by Hugh Benham, pages 37–39.

Tempo, metre and rhythm

- No tempo indications are given, as performers were expected to rely on time signatures and the general character of the music to sense the speed
- Movement 1 is in a form of cut common time (𝄵), but in this case the score was laid out with four (rather than two) minims per bar. This type of time signature indicated a brisk pace
- Quadruple time was used for movements 2 and 8
- In movement 2, the 'moto perpetuo' semiquavers with walking bass quavers and florid shorter values in vocal parts and oboe necessitates a relatively fast but controlled tempo
- In movement 8, a more moderate tempo is required. The Bach chorale typically relies heavily on flowing quavers in the lower parts. Notice that the pause marks indicate ends of phrases rather than significant lengthening of notes.

Melody

- Luther's chorale provides the melodic basis of all three movements to be studied

- Movement 8 presents the chorale tune without elaboration. Notice its
  - Powerful repeated notes
  - Mainly conjunct movement with just the occasional leap
  - Forceful descending scale at end of first section and again in the final phrase
  - Single note outside the scale of D major (G♯)
- In movement 1, each phrase is presented in turn. There is a very loose variation of the chorale melody in the vocal parts, a direct statement of the theme being reserved for the oboes in canon with violone
- Heavy ornamentation of the chorale melody occurs in movement 2
- Other points to note:
  - Sequence, e.g. cello in bar 1, movement 1
  - Chromaticism, movement 1, bars 97–99; word painting to underline the guile of the devil
  - The mixture of syllabic word-setting and grouping of two or three notes per syllable in the chorale
  - The extended melismas in the choral writing of movement 1, and bass solo of movement 2
  - The angular, almost instrumental writing for the bass singer, e.g. movement 2, bars 13–18.

Harmony

- Bach's harmony is functional, with:
  - Clearly defined cadences
  - Triads and 7ths in various positions
  - Pedal points, e.g. movement 1, bar 27^3 to bar 30^3
  - Suspensions, e.g. a 4–3 suspension in movement 8, bar 2^2; 7-6 suspension in movement 8, bar 8^1; 9-8 suspension, movement 8, bar 10^2
  - Dissonances arising from freely moving lines and passing notes
  - Diminished 7ths, e.g. movement 1, bar 71^{1-2}.

Tonality

- In movement 1, the chorale dominates throughout, meaning that the chorale's key (D major) is of major structural importance
- For variety, however, other related keys are employed, for example:
  - E minor (bars 63–64)

- B minor (bars 65–66)
- F♯ minor (bars 67–68)
- A major (bar 90)

- In movement 2, also in D major, there are again modulations to closely related keys, e.g. A major (bar 27), B minor (bar 46)
- Movement 8 provides insights into Bach's ingenious handling of a theme that could have been largely harmonised in D, e.g. perfect cadences in A major (bars 5 and 9) and imperfect cadence in E minor (bar 10).

Structure

Structures in the three prescribed movements are dictated by the chorale melody.

- Movement 1 takes each phrase in turn and presents it first in a fugal working-out in the vocal parts before rounding it off with a canonic version for oboes and violone
- Movement 2 uses ritornello form, i.e. a theme recurs at various points throughout the movement (upper strings), sometimes touching on different keys. Imposed on this scheme are statements of the chorale (soprano) with a different 'parallel' text in the bass
- Movement 8: a nine-line chorale, with repetitions (e.g. phrase 4 uses the same music as phrase 2, and phrase 9 has the same melodic line).

Texture

- Movement 1 is contrapuntal, with imitative writing in the vocal parts in fugal style, and canon at the octave in oboes and violone, with a half-bar between the entries
- The texture is further complicated by the heterophony in the cello at bars 20–22, where it plays a more elaborate version of the vocal bass line
- Movement 2 is also contrapuntal with a ritornello theme in upper strings, supported by a walking bass, over which can be heard an embellished version of the chorale in the soprano (with heterophony in the oboe part) and an independent line in the solo bass part
- Movement 8 is homophonic, though the lower parts are rhythmically independent.

FURTHER LISTENING

Listen to other works by Bach, e.g. the Brandenburg Concertos, Cantata No. 140, 'Wachet auf!', and also cantatas of a later period, such as Britten's St. Nicolas.

Die Zauberflöte, No. 4 (recit and aria: 'O zittre nicht') and No. 5 (quintet: 'Hm! Hm! Hm! Hm!) from Act 1 (Mozart)

Context

- This work is an example of a Classical-period opera
- *The Magic Flute (Die Zauberflöte)* is a Singspiel, a type of German language opera with spoken dialogue in place of the recitative that separates the arias, ensemble numbers and choruses in other types of opera. Recitative, which appears in No. 4, was reserved for the more dramatic moments
- First performed on 30 September, 1791
- It is a fantastical tale incorporating the ideals of the 18th century Enlightenment and Freemasonry
- It requires vocal soloists, chorus (though not in the prescribed extracts) and orchestra.

In No. 4, The Queen of the Night commands the hero, Tamino, to rescue her daughter, Pamina, from the clutches of the (supposed) villain, Sarastro. In No. 5, Papageno provides comic relief as he struggles with a gag placed on him by the Queen's attendants, the Three Ladies, as a punishment for lying. After he is freed, Tamino and Papageno are sent on their quest to rescue Pamina, protected respectively by a magic flute and bells, and guided by the Three Boys.

Sonority

- The soloists in these pieces are:
  - The Queen of the Night, sung by a high (coloratura) soprano
  - Tamino, a tenor
  - Papageno, a baritone
  - The Three Ladies, all of them soprano. They have separate parts, heard in homophony – though at bar 237, the first and second sopranos double at the unison
- Only part of the orchestra is required in these pieces: two oboes, two bassoons, two horns in B♭, and strings in No. 4, and the same forces plus clarinets in No. 5
- Pizzicato is used in the Andante in No. 5, bar 214 onwards.

Notation

- The music is presented as a vocal score with individual lines for each vocalist with the exception of the 1st and 2nd Ladies, whose parts are printed on the same stave
- Italian terms are used for tempos, even though the work uses the German language.

> Use of German for tempo indications was only introduced by Beethoven in his later works, in which both Italian and German directions are given.

- The usual (Italian) dynamic indications are used, though only rarely in the vocal parts (e.g. No. 5, bars 192–203)
- The direction 'sotto voce' ('under the voice') is used for the Three Ladies at bar 184 in No. 5
- In this score, German terms and abbreviations are used for the instruments, some of the less obvious terms are:
  - Br. for Bratsche (viola)
  - Bläs. for Bläser (wind instruments).

Tempo, metre and rhythm

- Both numbers contain tempo contrasts:
  - No. 4: Allegro maestoso – Larghetto – Allegro moderato
  - No. 5: Allegro – Moderato
- Metres also change:
  - No.4: simple quadruple ($\frac{4}{4}$) for the two allegro sections, contrasting with simple triple ($\frac{3}{4}$) in the Larghetto
  - No. 5: 'Cut common time' (fast two minims per bar) changing to more relaxed quadruple ($\frac{4}{4}$) in the Moderato
- Notice the following rhythmic features:
  - Syncopation in the orchestral introduction of No. 4, imparting a sense of urgency
  - The 'free time' delivery in the recitative section
  - Frequent dotted rhythms
  - Rapid, dramatic flourishes, e.g. the triplet semiquavers in the Allegro moderato (No. 4, bars 62–63)

- Virtuoso streams of semiquavers (No. 4, bars 79–92)
- Insertion of rests within melody of Andante (No. 5, bars 218–219).

Melody

- Overall the vocal range of 'The Queen of the Night's recitative and aria is wide, from D just above middle C, to F two octaves and a 3rd higher
- The last bar of the No. 4 Recitative contains a falling diminished 7th and a typical closing formula for recitatives, i.e. the falling 4th (see music example below)
- Unusual phrase structure at the start of the aria in No. 4, consisting of 3 + 3 + 2 + 2 bars
- Ornamentation and appoggiaturas intensify expressive power
- Sequence (No. 4, bars 28–31)
- Chromatic descent (No. 4, bars 41–43) for pathos
- Melody in the No. 4 Allegro moderato frequently contains rapidly moving scales
- Word-setting involves a mix of syllabic, slurred quavers and melismas
- Melody in the Quintet, No. 5 is marked by:
    - Periodic phrasing
    - Generally diatonic writing
    - Repeated notes.

Harmony

- Functional, with clearly defined perfect and imperfect cadences
- Interrupted cadences also appear, e.g. No. 4 bars 55–56
- Neapolitan 6th (No. 4, bar 19), followed by
- Diminished 7th (No. 4, bar 20)

No. 4, bars 18–21

- Tonic pedal at opening of No. 4
- Appoggiatura chord is used at bar 52 of No. 4
- Suspensions are rare, but see No. 4, bar 66[1]
- Notice the Augmented 6th chord in No. 5 at bar 150.

Augmented 6th

Tonality

- Both numbers are in the key of B♭ major and modulate to related keys, e.g.
    - G minor (No. 4, bar 21)
    - C minor (No. 4, bar 38)
    - F major (No. 5, bar 34)
    - D minor (No. 5, bar 142)
    - E♭ (No. 5, bar 172)

The five related keys in this instance are the dominant (F), subdominant (E♭), relative minor (G minor), and relative minors of the dominant (D minor) and subdominant (C minor).

Structure

- No. 4 is a recitative and aria
- In this case the recitative is orchestrally accompanied.

> Normally, dialogue in Singspiel was spoken, but accompanied recitative was sometimes used for scenes requiring heightened expression.

- The aria is in two sections, reflecting the developing dramatic situation:
  - Largo, in which the Queen of the Night expresses sorrow at the loss of her daughter and condemnation of Sarastro
  - Allegro moderato, in which Tamino is commanded to rescue Pamina
- No. 5 is a through-composed ensemble number with clearly differentiated sections that also reflect the course of the action.

Texture

- Mainly melody-dominated homophony (melody with accompaniment)
- Homophony (homorhythm), e.g. No. 5, bars 74–77
- Octaves, e.g. No. 5, bars 61–64.

FURTHER LISTENING

Beethoven's *Fidelio* and Weber's *Der Freischütz* are both examples of Singspiel. For an example of opera in which all sections are sung, see Mozart's *Marriage of Figaro* or *Don Giovanni*.

On Wenlock Edge, No. 1 'On Wenlock Edge', No. 3 'Is My Team Ploughing?' and No. 5 'Bredon Hill' (Vaughan Williams)

Context

- Vaughan Williams (1872–1958) was born in Down Ampney, Gloucestershire, and had family connections with the Wedgwood and Darwin dynasties
- He was educated at Charterhouse School, the Royal College of Music and Trinity Hall, Cambridge
- His principal teachers were Parry and Stanford, though he later sought tuition from Bruch (Berlin, 1897) and Ravel (Paris, 1908)
- He is celebrated in English music for his interest in folk music, undertaking folk-song collections in Essex, Norfolk and Sussex
- His early works reflect a gradual shift from a basically 'Romantic' approach (*Songs of Travel* and *Toward the Unknown Region*) to a style incorporating:
  - Folk influences, e.g. modality (*On Wenlock Edge*, 1908–09)
  - The influences of Tudor music (*Fantasia on a Theme of Thomas Tallis*, 1910)
  - Influences from Debussy and Ravel, notably harmonic parallelism, whole-tone harmony and colouristic sonorities
- ***On Wenlock Edge*** is a song-cycle consisting of six poems for tenor, string quartet and piano
  - It draws on verses from *A Shropshire Lad* by A. E. Housman (1859–1936)
  - Generally melancholy in tone, the subject matter often concerns mortality, the fleeting nature of life and thwarted love.

Notation

- The work is notated in open score with separate staves for the vocalist and each member of the string quartet; the piano uses the conventional two staves
- Vaughan Williams allowed for performance of the accompaniment on piano alone, providing an alternative part in small type at specific points, e.g. bars 31–38 of the first number
- An orchestral version was drawn up c. 1923
- Generally, Vaughan Williams uses Italian tempo directions though he resorts to English in 'Bredon Hill', e.g. 'to be sung freely' (bar 24) and the detailed instructions regarding dynamics (bar 100) and rhythm (bars 127 and 128).

No. 1 'On Wenlock Edge'

An evocation of a gale sweeping over Shropshire, buffeting the modern landscape just as it did the Romans 2000 years before. The wind will soon be gone, leading to the reflection that life's trials will end just as surely as those of the Roman, now 'ashes under Uricon'.

Sonority

- The vocalist's range (notated in treble clef, but sounding an octave lower than written) is D below middle C, to G above middle C
- Stringed instruments avoid extreme ranges, the highest pitch in violin I being E♭ just over two octaves above middle C, in the recurring motif first heard in bars 1–3
- Other effects include:
  - Pizzicato, in cello only (both single notes and triple-stopped chords)
  - Multiple stopping only occurs in the cello part
  - Tremolo (single notes and rapid alternations between pitches), representing the gale
  - Lengthy trills applied with colouristic effect (bars 31–32)
  - Sul ponticello (bowing near the bridge) used to produce a thin, harsh quality (bar 57)
- Apart from conventional chords and broken chord passages on piano, there are also:
  - Colouristic washes of sound (bar 31)
  - Long trills (bars 33–38)
  - Tremolos (bars 67–75)
- The piano occasionally carries the melody, e.g. at bar 7 where it doubles the tenor, and at bars 62–64 where it is independent
- In spite of the song's subject, the dynamic level never rises above f. Notice also:
  - Sudden crescendos and diminuendos
  - p marks (bar 28)
  - ppp marking at bar 32
  - $pppp$ with diminuendo at bars 76–77
  - Accent signs (bar 3, piano LH).

Texture

The song is homophonic throughout, though with considerable variety in use of voice and instruments:

Bar 1	Chordal, with tremolo effects
Bar 3	String trills doubled at the octave with piano RH broken chords, reinforced with block chords in LH
Bar 7	Piano broken chords continue in RH, but LH now doubles the tenor and cello melody; string trills continue in violin II and viola
Bar 31	String trills over three octaves with 'impressionistic' washes of sound in piano
Bar 35	Piano trills in both hands an octave apart, vocal monotone and parallel chords in strings
Bar 41	Broken chord first inversions in piano, violin I shadows tenor line in heterophony
Bar 57	Tenor accompanied by tremolo in three upper string parts sul ponticello
Bar 62	Tenor accompanied by piano with independent melody in LH and chords in RH; tremolo in three upper strings ('naturale', i.e. bowed normally) with sustained notes in cello

Tempo, metre and rhythm

- **Tempo** is Allegro moderato, the effect of the gale indicated by agitato, and its subsiding by tranquillo (bar 62 to the end)
- **Metre** is simple quadruple ($\frac{4}{4}$) throughout
- **Rhythm** plays an important part in establishing the stormy atmosphere:
  - Prominent triplets and sextuplets (e.g. opening section)
  - Forcefully articulated rhythm with effect of dotted rhythm in which the dot is replaced with a semiquaver rest (e.g. bars 3–5):

Bars 3–5 (piano only)

- Demisemiquaver scale at bar 12
- Hemidemisemiquavers in piano at bar 31
- Off-beat entries in strings at bar 35.

Melody

- Word-setting is predominantly syllabic, the exceptions being two slurred notes on the first syllable of 'Wrekin' at bar 10, and three notes slurred on 'heav-' (bar 37) and 'gale' (bar 48)
- Other note-worthy features of the vocal line include:
  - Pentatonic lines (e.g. bars 6–10)

Bars 6–10

  - Monotone passages (bars 11–12 and 34–35)
  - Chromaticism (bars 13–16)

Bars 11–16

- Diminished 5th leap (e.g. 'ashes under Uricon' at bars 67–68)

Bars 67–68

- The instruments occasionally share the vocalist's material, but their most important motif is the recurring figure, first heard in the opening bars. It moves down then up through a 5th and is harmonised in first inversion chords.

Harmony

This number is largely devoid of functional chord progressions, although repeated dominant-tonic notes are heard in the bass (bars 71–77) to bring the song to a close.

Notice in particular:

- Parallel first inversion chords at the opening
- The false relation which appears at the close of this opening motif (D♭–D♮):

Bars 1–3 (piano only)

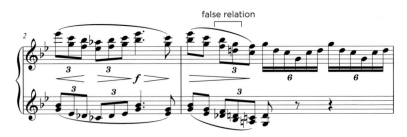

- Parallel root position chords (without 5ths) at bar 35:

Bars 35-36

- Largely whole-tone figuration in piano at bars 43–44: notice that apart from the F♭ at the top of the pattern, the remaining notes all belong to a single whole-tone scale
- Closes with dissonant passage with clashing G and A♭, before fading out with open 5ths and dominant to tonic octaves.

Tonality and structure

The song opens as if 'strophic', i.e. with repeated verses, but introduces new material and eventually fuses the various thematic elements. It is in G (modal) minor, though the basic key is not established through functional progressions.

Bars 1-6	Introduction	Motif (a), strings and piano	Region of E♭ moving to tonality 'on', rather than in, G (NB chords here are built on G, C and D
Bars 6-16	Stanza 1 ('On Wenlock Edge')	(b)	G pentatonic, closing on E♭⁷ (with D♭ in bass). Some bitonality with A♭ melody in bass at bar 11

Bars 16–21	Link 1: intro repeated	(a)	
Bars 21–31	Stanza 2 ('Twould blow like this')	(b)	G pentatonic – E♭⁷
Bars 31–33	Link 2 (trills and whole-tone flourishes)		
Bars 34–43	Stanza 3 ('Then, 'twas before my time')	(c1) and (c2)	Unstable area: starts and finishes on E♭⁷ with chromatically descending first inversion chords in between
Bars 43–44	Link 2		
Bars 45–55	Stanza 4 ('There like the wind')	(c) varied	Descending first inversion chords now heard a semitone higher
Bars 55–57	Link 1	(a)	
Bars 58–68	Stanza 5 ('The gale, it plies the saplings double')	(b)	G pentatonic with bitonal A♭ bass; 'Uricon' harmonised with whole tone chord (bar 68, beat 3)
Bars 69–77	Coda	(c1) fused with (b)	Shifts to G pentatonic, closing with open 5ths chord

No. 3 'Is My Team Ploughing?'

This number, the third of the six forming the song cycle, is a dialogue between a ghost and his still-living friend, during which it becomes clear that the friend has taken over the dead man's girl as his lover.

Sonority

- Ranges:
  - Tenor: D below middle C to A above middle C
  - Violin I: highest note is B♮, almost three octaves above middle C
  - Cello: B just over an octave below middle C to the B above middle C, the highest pitch being deployed at the climax
- String techniques:
  - Pizzicato in cello only (bars 37 and 41)
  - Mutes (con sord.) used in all instruments at various points
  - Tremolo (e.g. bar 37)
- Use of piano:
  - Silent at opening, bars 19–26 and 57–62
  - Triplet chords (typical 'Romantic' idiom) e.g. at bars 9–16
  - Tremolo (e.g. bar 39)
  - Una corda specified in the piano-only version
- Dynamics range from *pp* (including *pp* quasi da lontano [as if from afar]) to *ff* (bar 50).

Texture

The song effectively contrasts unaccompanied strings (as at the opening) with textures involving the piano.

The number uses various homophonic and melody-dominated homophonic textures:

Bars 1–4	Chords in three upper strings (muted)
Bars 5–8	Sustained three-note D minor chord supports freely moving tenor melody
Bars 9–16	Piano chords with bass doubled by cello; in bars 13–17 the cello shadows the vocalist in heterophony
Bars 19–21	Original three-part string texture expanded with addition of single cello note
Bars 37–44	Piano doubles string chords; tremolo applied in all parts
Bar 50	Piano triplet chords and string octaves accompany tenor
Bars 51–53	Voice accompanied by just piano in octaves

Tempo, metre and rhythm

- A flexible scheme is used regarding **tempo**, with movement from Andante sostenuto ma non troppo lento (for the ghost's opening question) to animando and poco animato for the replies. As the number approaches the climax, the direction is Poco più mosso with an allargando at 'dead man's sweet-heart'. Additional terms include misterioso, quasi da lontano, agitato and affretando
- The **metre** is basically quadruple time ($\frac{4}{4}$), with some $\frac{3}{4}$ and $\frac{2}{4}$ bars inserted
- **Rhythm** is relatively free, sometimes to the extent that pulse is disguised, e.g. the introduction with its mix of dotted rhythm, tied notes, triplets, syncopations and long sustained notes. Elsewhere, notice:
  - The lengthening of note-values at the ends of phrases (e.g. bar 8 – see example below), leading to a change of time signature
  - Triplet quavers in piano accompaniment (bar 9)
  - Quintuplets (e.g. cello in bar 12)
  - Septuplets (e.g. cello in bar 45).

Melody

- Word-setting is predominantly syllabic, the exceptions being two slurred notes on the two words 'used to' (bar 6), and at corresponding points later in the song: 'hard to' (bar 24), and 'thin and' (bar 40)

- The opening, folk-like melody is in dorian mode (notice the B♮s within a scale starting on D):

Bars 5–9

- A more complex melodic style is used for the 'reply', with chromaticism and larger leaps:

Bars 11–19

- Higher tessitura is used in the final stanzas, rising to A above middle C on 'dead' (bar 50)

- Final note in vocal part is B♮, clashing with the tonic triad which follows.

Harmony

■ Introductory music draws on root and first inversion chords only, and features some parallelism:

Bars 1–3

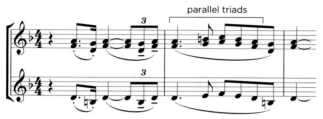

■ The passage beginning at bar 11 is more complex, and includes:

   ■ Augmented triad (bars 11^4 and 13^4)

   ■ Half-diminished chord (bars 12^1 and 14^1)

   ■ 'Neapolitan' chord (bar 15^1)

   ■ Augmented ('French') 6th (bar 15^2)

   ■ Fourths chord (bar 16^1):

Bars 13–16 (piano only)

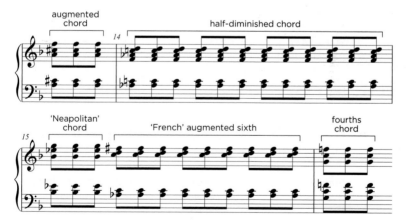

Structure and tonality

- The structure is a sort of expanded strophic, with substantial repetitions of material
- Tonality starts and closes in D dorian minor, moving into a more Romantic chromatic language which clouds the key at some points.

Bars 1–4	Introduction	A1	D dorian
Bars 5–9	Stanza 1 ('Is my team')	A2, expanding on A1	D dorian
Bars 9–19	Stanza 2 ('Ay, the horses')	B	D minor, chromatic progressions lead to G♯ half-diminished before voice closes on A
Bars 19–22	Link (repeat of opening)	A1	D dorian, with added G in bass
Bars 23–27	Stanza 3 ('Is my girl')	A2	D dorian
Bars 27–37	Stanza 4 ('Ay, she lies')	B	D minor, as in bars 9–19
Bars 37–38	Link shortened	A1	D dorian
Bars 39–44	Stanza 5 ('Is my friend')	A2 transposed 4th higher	D dorian – F minor
Bars 45–55	Stanza 6 ('Yes, lad')	Vocal departs from previous material (stress on falling minor 2nd) but piano retains the triplet chord textures	Indeterminate, but moves towards E
Bars 55–62	Coda (based on intro)	A1	D dorian

No. 5 'Bredon Hill'

For the fifth of the six songs making up *On Wenlock Edge*, the scene is not in fact Shropshire, but the borders of Worcestershire and Gloucestershire, hence the reference to the bells ringing 'round both the shires'.

Lovers lie on Bredon Hill, ignoring the bells calling them to church on a summer Sunday morning. They will go when the bells call them to their wedding. Alas, the girl dies in winter and goes to church alone, summoned by a single tolling bell.

Vaughan Williams's debt to Ravel is at its clearest in this song, particularly in terms of piano sonorities which recall similar bell effects in Ravel's *Miroirs*, No. 5 ('La vallée des cloches'), dating from 1904–05.

Sonority

- Ranges:
  - Tenor: from E♭ sounding a 6th below middle C, to A a 6th above
  - Piano has a five octave range, extending upwards from the G two and a half octaves below middle C
  - Stringed instruments exploit relatively high ranges through the use of harmonics
- String techniques:
  - Pizzicato in violin I only (bars 100–109) to reinforce the effect of the tolling funeral bell
  - Mutes (con sord.) used in all instruments at various points
  - Double stopping increases the density of the sounds
  - Tremolo (e.g. bars 123–130)
  - Succession of down bows for emphasis (violin II and viola, bars 128–133): see example below under 'melody'
  - Harmonics applied at various points, e.g. bar 114
- Use of piano:
  - Extensive passage for piano alone accompanying voice (bars 52–83)
  - Triplet parallel 5th and octave chords for pealing bell effects (e.g. bars 52–79); elsewhere parallel 4ths (bar 20)
  - Extensive use of both una corda and sustaining pedal simultaneously (e.g. opening)
  - Limited use of tremolo (see bar 123)
- **Dynamics** range from *pppp* (bar 20) to *ff* in all parts (bar 127).

Texture

Homophonic or melody-dominated homophonic textures predominate, although there is considerable variety in their handling:

Bar 1	Block chords (homophony/homo-rhythm)
Bar 20	Sustained chord combined with parallel 4ths in imitation; the effect is primarily colouristic rather than contrapuntal
Bar 24	Sustained chord as backdrop to freely moving vocal melody
Bar 52	Piano only: sustained LH chords, some widely spaced (up to a span of a 10th); RH in parallel octaves and 5ths, or else 4ths (bar 64)
Bar 100	Funeral march with tolling bell represented by a combination of pizzicato octave in violin I, arco octave in violin II, piano octave in middle range; remainder of texture made up of parallel 5ths and octave chords in RH supported by LH 7th chords
Bar 105	Bass line in cello and viola with LH piano added above
Bar 115	Harmonics in three upper strings with broken (7th) chords in piano
Bar 123	Staccato quavers in violins I and II combined with tremolo viola, reinforced by broken chords figuration in piano
Bar 127	'Wild bells' effect with tremolo strings, RH broken chords, LH chord, heavily accented octaves descending by step in violin II, viola and middle range of piano, supporting the rhythmically independent vocal line

Tempo, metre and rhythm

- **Tempo** is flexible with frequent changes to underline the course of the narrative, e.g. Moderato tranquillo (bar 1), Poco animato (bar 52), animato (bar 58), molto tranquillo (bar 64), Più lento (bar 84), largamente (bar 100), Tempo alla prima (bar 136)
  - There are further slight fluctuations, e.g. accel. – rit. (bars 21–22)
- **Metre** also varies:
  - Simple duple ($\frac{2}{2}$) with occasional departures, e.g. one bar of $\frac{2}{4}$ at bar 32 and one bar of $\frac{3}{2}$ at bar 71
  - The metre changes to $\frac{4}{4}$ at bar 84, underlining the slackening of pace to emphasise the more solemn mood, and this signature continues into the 'funeral' music at bar 100
  - A return to $\frac{2}{2}$ at bar 115 and at the closing passage (bar 136), with the intervening section that leads to the climax (from bar 123) in $\frac{4}{4}$
- Notice the following **rhythmic** features:
  - Long, spacious time-values establish the calm of the opening
  - Vocal melody, 'to be sung freely', contains the occasional triplet quaver group
  - Persistent triplet (crotchets) at bar 56
  - Cross-rhythms appear between piano and vocal line in the passage from bar 52
  - Ponderous dotted rhythms and off-beat 'tolling' effect contribute to funereal atmosphere at bar 100
  - Urgency of the bells' summons at bar 123 underlined by the quaver motor rhythms
  - Vocal line at bar 128 to be sung 'quite freely', irrespective of the strict times maintained in the accompanying parts, giving rise to an aleatoric effect
  - At this point, piano and strings introduce a triplet figure which appears every third beat producing a cross-rhythmic effect (see example given under 'melody').

Melody

- Word-setting is mainly syllabic, with the occasional slurrings (e.g. first syllable of 'Bredon' at bar 26
- Melisma is used for special emphasis, e.g. the hectoring quality on 'pray' at bars 62–63
- The melody is in G pentatonic major at the outset, but the wider range of notes from bar 29 results in mixolydian mode, and at bar 33, aeolian mode:

Bars 24–35

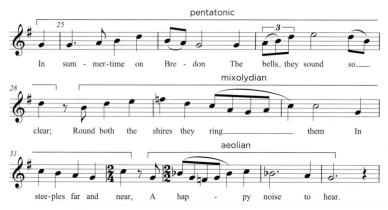

- Mainly step movement, with occasional leaps, e.g. perfect 4th (bars 55–56), descending major 6th (bars 56–57), descending minor 7th (bars 69–70), octave (bar 77)

- Range of melody narrows for the funeral music, with a prominent secondary motive spanning a 3rd

- This narrow range motif is treated chromatically, e.g. bars 96–100:

Bars 92–100

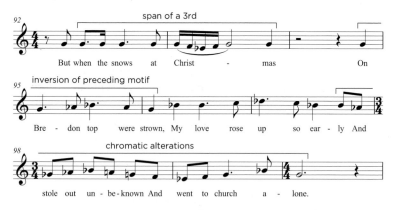

- Notable instrumental motifs include:

  - A foreshadowing of the vocal line at bars 9–10 (compare pitches with those of vocal line at bars 25–26):

Bars 9–10 (violin I)

- A line in the piano part, largely restricted to interval of a 2nd for the funeral music:

Bars 100–101 (piano only)

- A distraught descending triplet (piano and strings) in reaction to the 'noisy bells':

Bars 128–130 (violin II)

Harmony

The harmony of this number is the least traditional of the three songs which are prescribed for study, and again Vaughan Williams's debt to Ravel is evident, particularly in the use of harmony for colouristic effect and avoidance of functional progression.

- Use of 7th chords which, when superimposed, result in chords of an 11th
- Colouristic overlapping parallel 4ths heard against a prolonged 11th chord:

Bars 20–23 (piano only)

- 7ths are sometimes inverted (see bar 29)
- Static or slow moving progressions: see the harmonies supporting the voice at bars 24–35
- Tension heightened at bar 84 onwards when the A♮ becomes an A♭, underpinning a thinned-out structure which still, overall, spans an 11th:

Bars 84–85 (piano only)

diminished 11th

- Bitonal structures based on A♭ and G dominate the funeral music section: see the above example for bars 100–101 under 'melody'.

Structure and tonality

Tonality is largely in/on G, though with varying modal inflections and an avoidance of cadential harmony. The structure is strophic in the early stages, eventually becoming more through-composed.

Bars 1–24	Instrumental introduction, foreshadowing vocal motifs and introducing parallel 4ths		G, but with prominent A^{11} chord
Bars 24–35	Stanza 1: 'In summertime'	(a)	G pentatonic, broadening to G mixolydian and G aeolian
Bars 35–38	Link (based on introduction)		A^{11}
Bars 39–48	Stanza 2: 'Here of a Sunday morning'	(a)	As before, with slight variation in harmonic scheme
Bars 48–51	Link (slightly varied)		A^{11}

Bars			
Bars 52–66	Stanza 3: 'The bells would ring'	(b)	$B\flat$ in voice, supported by C^{11} moving to $E\flat^{7}$ before closing on $B^{7}d$, bringing a return to the original atmosphere
Bars 66–78	Stanza 4: 'And I would turn'	(b)2	$B^{7}d \longrightarrow A^{11}$
Bars 79–83	Link with parallel 4ths		A^{11}
Bars 84–92	Introduction to funeral music		Thinned out $A\flat^{11}$, bringing bitonal elements into play
Bars 92–100	Stanza 5: 'But when the snows'	(c)	G minor $\longrightarrow$ $B\flat$ minor, with chromatic alterations
Bars 100–113	Stanza 6: 'They tolled the bell'	(c)2	G minor $\longrightarrow$ $B\flat$ minor with bitonal support and prominent tolling pedal G
Bars 114–135	Stanza 7: 'The bells they sound'	(a)	Tonality as for stanza 1, but with harmonic framework extended
Bars 136–46	Coda, derived from introduction		A^{11}, with monotone G for final vocal entry

FURTHER LISTENING

You might like to investigate other relatively early works by Vaughan Williams, such as *Fantasia on a Theme of Thomas Tallis* and Symphony No. 2 (the 'London' Symphony). Try also Elgar's *Sea Pictures*, Ravel's *Trois poèmes de Stéphane Mallarmé*, Schoenberg's *Pierrot Lunaire* and Britten's *Les Illuminations* and *Serenade for tenor, horn and strings*.

AREA OF STUDY 2:

Instrumental music

Concerto in D minor Op. 3 No. 11 RV 565 (Vivaldi)

Context

- Late Baroque
- Concerto grosso: a work for a group of soloists (concertino) – in this case two violins and a cello – supported by a group of string players and harpsichord/organ continuo
- Vivaldi was an Italian (Venetian) composer. This work was published in Amsterdam in 1711 as one of the 12 concertos that form *L'estro Armonico* ('*Harmonic Fancy*' or '*Harmonic Inspiration*')
- The exact date of composition cannot be established and it might have been much earlier than the date of publication.

Sonority and performance forces

- Three solo strings with a larger accompanying group including continuo – a 'cembalo' (harpsichord) and a violone (equivalent of a double bass)
- The strings are bowed throughout
- Violin range extends up to D, just over two octaves above middle C
- Solo cello extends to G above middle C
- Resonant exploitation of open strings at the start of the work
- Contrast of forces plays an essential part throughout
- The central part of the slow (third) movement (Largo e spiccato) is for upper strings only; the bass instruments and continuo rest at this point.

Note that contrasts in performing forces had played a major role in Venetian music for over a century before Vivaldi. See works by Giovanni Gabrieli and Claudio Monteverdi.

Notation

- The version printed in the Anthology is a full score with each part allotted its own line
- The Anthology score does not differentiate between soloists and ripieno, but Violins I and II are soloists, and III and IV are ripieno. The solo cello line is on the stave above the continuo
- Typical Baroque features of the score include:
  - Figured bass – a system of harmonic shorthand, which conveyed to the keyboard player the chords to be supplied. Figures indicate the intervals above the bass. The indication 'Tasto solo' (see movement 2, bar 58) means that only the bass line, without chords, is to be played at this point
  - Dynamics are 'terraced' – bold, abrupt contrasts between loud and soft. There are no crescendo or diminuendo marks; mid-volume dynamics, such as *mp* and *mf*, are avoided
  - Italian indications are performance instructions, e.g. *spiccato* (detached bow strokes).

Tempo, metre and rhythm

Tempo

- According to the Anthology, the concerto consists of four main sections: Allegro – brief 'Adagio e spiccato' leading to Allegro – Largo e spiccato – Allegro

Metre

- The first movement (Allegro) is in $\frac{3}{4}$
- The second movement (Adagio e spiccato; Allegro) is in common time in both sections
- The third movement (Largo e spiccato) is in compound quadruple ($\frac{12}{8}$) time
- The fourth movement – Allegro – returns to common time.

Rhythm

- Movements I, II and IV are characterised by typically Baroque 'motor' rhythms, i.e. hard-driven patterns, helped along by the almost percussive harpsichord continuo
- Movement I opens with continuous quavers, leading to running semiquavers
- The short Adagio section at the start of movement II is rhythmically simple with four even quavers followed by a minim with pause
- Movement III draws on rocking Siciliano rhythms.

Melody

- Broken chord patterns in opening bars of first movement (I)
- Scales (descending at II, bar 13, and inverted to rise at II, bar 37)
- Sequences are frequent, e.g. II, bars 25–26
- Leaps, e.g. 5ths at II, bars 25–26 and 7th at III, bar 4
- Chromatic, e.g. IV, bars 4–6
- Ornaments are confined to the occasional trill.

Harmony

- Functional, with strong drive to cadences
- Vocabulary draws on root position chords, first inversions and 7ths
- Frequent circles of 5ths (II, bars 33–35)
- Suspensions, e.g. 4–3 at II, bar 50
- An unusual false relation occurs at II, bar 3 (i.e. E♭ in C minor chord followed by E♮ in a different part of the succeeding A major chord)
- Neapolitan 6th chord, e.g. III, bar 2^2
- Diminished 7th, III, bar 5^2
- Dominant pedal at II, bars 58–69.

Tonality

- Vivaldi uses a tonal scheme based on functional harmonies, defined by cadences
- This system of functional tonality allows modulations
- The tonic key of all three movements is D minor
- Vivaldi modulates mainly to related keys:
    - A minor (II, bar 32)
    - G minor (II, bar 48)
    - F major (II, bar 52)
- Unusually, Vivaldi moves to the unrelated key of F minor in III, bars 7–8
- Other devices used to underline tonality include:
    - Circle of 5ths progressions (e.g. II, bars 33–35)
    - Dominant pedal (see bars 58–69 at end of the second movement)
    - Tierce de Picardie (II, bar 70), which unusually leads to a conclusion in the tonic minor.

Structure

- Movement I: bars 1–31
- Movement II: introductory Adagio (bars 1–3) leading to Allegro (bars 4–73)
    - In the allegro starting at bar 4, fugal textures are coordinated within a scheme of contrasting tutti-solo sections
    - Though not a complete fugue, it is appropriate to use fugal terminology in describing the start of the Allegro:
    - Subject – the theme announced in the bass in the tonic at bar 4
    - Answer – the second entry of the theme, now in the dominant (viola at bar 8)
    - Countersubject – the 'countermelody' to the answer in the bass at bar 8
    - Countersubject 2 – an additional counterpoint to both subject and counter-subject (bass, bar 12)
- Movement III is in ternary form (A–B–A)
- Movement IV is in a loose ritornello form. The recurring ritornello theme embraces both solo and tutti sections, and is identifiable by reference to motifs at bars 1, 7 and 11.

The basic outline of the movement is as follows:

Bar 1	Ritornello	D minor
Bar 14	Episode	
Bar 19	Ritornello	A minor
Bar 30	Episode	
Bar 53	Ritornello (shortened)	D minor
Bar 59	Episode	
Bar 68	Ritornello (final motif)	D minor

Texture

- Movement I opens with a two-part canon at the distance of a crotchet beat, lengthening at bar 6 to a bar between imitations. The passage at bar 20 is a cello melody with continuo accompaniment

- The Adagio at the start of movement II is homophonic

- The Allegro from bar 4 of movement II is fugal

- Movement III is melody-dominated homophony, with lower strings and continuo omitted in the central section

- Movement IV is contrapuntal at the opening, but other passages are more homophonic. In these sections, notice the differentiation between accompaniments of crotchet chords followed by crotchet rest (bar 7) and those with continuous quavers (bar 36).

FURTHER LISTENING

You could refer to other Baroque composers of concerti grossi, e.g. Corelli, Handel and J. S. Bach. In more recent times, comparisons could be drawn with Stravinsky (*Dumbarton Oaks*) and Tippett (Concerto for Double String Orchestra).

Piano Trio in G minor, Op. 17: movement 1 (Clara Schumann)

Context

- Romantic era work, completed in 1846

- A piano trio is a chamber work with parts for violin, cello and piano, popularised by Haydn and taken up by composers such as Mozart, Beethoven, Brahms and Shostakovich

- This trio has four movements, but you are only required to study the first movement

- Clara Schumann: daughter of Friedrich Wieck, a celebrated piano teacher; wife of composer Robert Schumann. She was one of a limited number of 19th-century women composers, other near contemporaries being Fanny Mendelssohn, sister of composer Felix Mendelssohn, and Maria Szymanowska.

Sonority

- All three instruments are treated in a conventional manner
- Ranges are well within each instrument's capabilities: nearly three octaves for violin and cello, and five and a half octaves for piano
- Limited use of pizzicato in cello, e.g. bars 238–246
- Double-stopping in violin, e.g. bars 21–23
- Piano pedalling indications are rare.

Notation

- The two stringed instruments are allotted a stave each, their parts printed above the piano's two staves
- When leaving the lower ranges, notated in bass clef, the cello part is printed in treble clef (not tenor), sounding an octave lower than written (see bar 122)
- Dynamics range between *ff* and *p*, with frequent use of crescendos and diminuendos
- Tempo indications are Italian.

Tempo, metre and rhythm

Tempo

- Allegro moderato, though the metronome mark of 152 crotchets per minute is relatively brisk
- Changes in tempo are rare, notably 'poco rit.' (bar 56 and 220), although the 'animato' at bar 266 invites an increase of pace to approach the end

Metre

- Common time throughout

Rhythm

- Persistent quaver movement
- Syncopation (e.g. bars 39–40)
- Forceful dotted rhythms.

Melody

- Balanced phrases
- Sequential repetition (e.g. bars 14–17)
- Melodic leaps in the violin part include: augmented 4th (bar 25), minor 6th (bar 29), minor 7th (bars 29–30)

- Opening violin melody is marked by strong perfect 5ths (bar 1) and leap of an octave (bar 6)
- Use of appoggiatura to intensify expressive effect (e.g. bar 7[1], violin)
- Chromaticism (e.g. strings, bars 66–67).

Harmony

- Clara Schumann's harmony is functional and marked by a strong drive towards cadences:
  - Imperfect, bar 4
  - Perfect, bars 21–22
  - Plagal, bars 285–286
- Suspensions, e.g. bar 18
- Chromatic chords:
  - Neapolitan 6th (bar 191)
  - Diminished 7th (bar 13[2])
  - French augmented 6th (bar 11[4])
- Anticipation (bar 5[4], violin)
- Dominant pedal (bars 155–164, cello).

Structure and tonality

The movement is in sonata form and for the most part modulates to related keys:

Exposition (repeated) bars 1–90		
Bars 1–21	1st subject	G minor
Bars 22–45	Bridge	
Bars 45–85	2nd subject	B♭ major
Bars 85–90	Codetta	Transitioning back to G minor

Development bars 91–164 (based largely on 1st subject)		
C minor (bar 92–94)		
Eb (bar 107)		
F minor (bar 111)		
C minor (from bar 127)		
G minor (from bar 150) with dominant pedal from bar 155		

Recapitulation bars 165–249		
Bars 165–185	1st subject	G minor
Bars 186–210	Bridge	
Bars 210–249	2nd subject	G major
Bars 250–288	Coda	G minor

Texture

- Mainly homophonic (e.g. bars 21–23) or melody-dominated homophony (e.g. bars 1–8)
- Some contrapuntal exchanges between violin and cello, from bar 115
- Melodic interest is usually kept in the violin or right hand of piano
- Cello reinforces violin line in octaves (bar 47) or in 10ths (from bar 17)
- Piano part is often made up of broken chords (maintaining a flow of quavers) or is chordal (bar 41).

FURTHER LISTENING

Useful comparisons could be made with works by Beethoven (Archduke Trio), Brahms (Piano Trio No. 3), Dvořák (Dumky Trio) and Shostakovich (Piano Trio No. 2).

Symphonie fantastique: movement 1 (Berlioz)

Context

- Hector Berlioz (1803–69) was born in La Côte-Saint-André near Grenoble and died in Paris
- He is regarded as the leading French Romantic composer of the first part of the 19th century, associating with leading artistic figures of the times, notably the composers Mendelssohn, Chopin and Liszt (who made a piano transcription of *Symphonie fantastique*); the writers, Victor Hugo, Dumas, Heine and Balzac; and the painters Delacroix and Ingres
- Unusually for his time he had no keyboard skills, playing only guitar and flute; this may have had an influence on his harmonic writing and the pronounced melodic and lyrical aspects of his music
- His works reveal a mastery of orchestral sonorities and considerable originality in his handling of established genres. Notable examples of his work, include:
  - The symphony *Harold in Italy*, with viola obbligato, written for Paganini (1834)
  - *Roméo et Juliette*, a dramatic symphony for voices and orchestra (1839)
  - *Grande symphonie funèbre et triomphale* for military band (1840)
  - The overtures, *Le carnaval romain* (1844) and *Le corsaire* (1844)
  - The operas *Les Troyens* (1858) and *Béatrice et Bénédict* (1862)
  - The choral works *Grande messe des morts [Requiem]* (1837), *La damnation de Faust* (1846) and *L'enfance du Christ* (1854)
- Berlioz toured widely, conducting his own works
- Many of his compositions reflect his literary interests, and he was a pioneer in the writing of programmatic music, a hallmark of the Romantic era
- He was also one of the earliest composers (along with Schumann) to write a considerable amount of music criticism
- Other important writings include:
  - *Grand traité d'instrumentation et d'orchestration modernes* (1844)
  - *Mémoires* (published 1870).

Symphonie fantastique

- This work was composed very quickly in early 1830 and first performed at the Paris Conservatoire on 5 December the same year

- Though retaining the broad outlines of the Classical symphony, Berlioz's work was extended from the usual four movements to five

- It came at a time in his career when he was responding to a number of experiences, personal, musical and literary:

  - His infatuation with the Irish actress, Harriet Smithson

  - Shakespeare's plays

  - Beethoven's symphonies

  - Goethe's *Faust*

- It is notable as an expression of the Romantic spirit sweeping Europe:

  - It is programmatic, i.e. it tells a story, in this case the partly autobiographical 'Episode in the life of an artist', intended as a reproach to Harriet for ignoring the composer's advances

  - Its use of an expanded orchestra (two harps, cor anglais, E♭ clarinet, bells, ophicleide – a rather unreliable bass trombone which Berlioz subsequently replaced with tuba)

  - Use of special effects, e.g. the off-stage oboe in the third movement, woodwind glissandi and col legno (strings playing with the wood of the bow) in the fifth movement

  - The innovative approach to formal design, with an *idée fixe*, a recurring musical theme which symbolises the loved one. This theme is subjected to considerable variation, depending on the programmatic content, and the underlying method is a striking anticipation of the metamorphosis of themes to be found in Liszt's works and the leitmotif technique of Wagner

- The symphony drew on a number of Berlioz's earlier works:

  - The theme at bar 3 of the first movement was taken from a setting of Florian's 'Je vais donc quitter pour jamais' from *Estelle et Némorin*

  - The *idée fixe* (starting in bar 71) came from *Herminie*, a cantata written in 1828

  - The fourth movement was originally 'March of the Guards', from the opera *Les Francs Juges* (1826)

- You are required to study only the first movement, but it would be rewarding to become acquainted with the whole symphony and its underlying narrative:

  1. **Rêveries – Passions**: 'The composer imagines that a young musician [...] sees for the first time a woman who possesses all the charms of the ideal being he has dreamed of, and falls desperately in love with her [...]

The transition from a state of dreamy melancholy, interrupted by several fits of aimless joy, to one of delirious passion, with its impulses of rage and jealousy, its returning moments of tenderness, its tears, and its religious solace, is the subject of the first movement' (Eulenberg Score 442).

2. **Un bal (Scene at a ball)**: fleeting vision of the beloved, bringing trouble to the artist's soul.

3. **Scène aux champs (In the country)**: the artist muses on his loneliness.

4. **Marche au supplice (March to the scaffold)**: The artist poisons himself with opium and dreams that he has killed his beloved and is being taken to his execution.

5. **Songe d'une nuit du sabbat (Dream of a witches' sabbath)**: The artist dreams he is at his own funeral, the rites conducted by witches including his beloved, her theme now hideously distorted. The plainsong *Dies irae* is also parodied.

Notation

Symphonie fantastique **is notated in the form of a full orchestral score, with a stave for each instrument presented in the usual way, that is woodwind instruments at the top, then brass, percussion and strings at the bottom:**

- The complete band used in this movement is shown at the start (apart from the piccolo (la petite flûte) which is taken up by one of the flautists at bar 401 and starts playing at 409

- Subsequently systems vary in size depending on the number of instruments required at any one moment

- Each woodwind instrument is allotted one stave, on which both parts are printed

- The four horns are allotted two staves, and trumpets and cornets à pistons one each

- Violin I and violin II are printed on two separate staves, as is normal

- A number of instruments are transposing, i.e. they are notated at a pitch different from the concert pitch the listener hears. In the case of woodwind instruments, a different key signature will be used, but in older orchestral scores such as this, brass instruments are printed without key signature

- Remember that in relation to the printed pitch

  - Clarinet in B♭ sounds a tone lower

  - Horn in E♭ sounds a major 6th lower

  - Horn in C sounds an octave lower

  - Cornets à pistons are notated in G and therefore sound a perfect 4th lower

  - Double bass sounds an octave lower

- Berlioz uses conventional dynamic marks, although the last section, starting at bar 511, has the additional comment in French '*Tout l'orchestre aussi doux que possible*' (all the orchestra as soft as possible)
- A mixture of Italian and French is used for tempo indications, e.g. the opening of the movement is marked Largo but as the music unfolds we see such directions as 'plus vite', 'animez', 'un peu plus vite', 'retenu jusqu'au premier movement', and so on
- Italian is used for stringed instrument techniques: 'con sord.', 'pizz.', 'arco', but French for instructions to the timpanist: 'baguettes de bois recouvert en peau' (hard sticks) and 'baguettes d'éponge' (felt sticks).

Sonority

The most striking orchestral innovations occur in the later movements, e.g. the two harps in the second movement, cor anglais and additional timpani used chordally in the third movement, chords for double bass in the fourth movement and the woodwind glissandi, bells and col legno (wood of the bow) playing of strings in the finale.

In comparison, the instrumentation for the first movement appears comparatively straightforward, but notice:

- The large string section specified (at least 15 first violins, 15 second violins, 10 violas, 11 cellos and 9 double basses)
- The use of four rather than the usual two bassoons
- The addition of cornets à pistons (valved brass instruments capable of playing chromatic notes).

The handling of these forces is distinguished for its contrasts of timbres and comparatively transparent sounds.

Notice the following:

- Contrast of woodwind and horns (bars 1-2) with strings (bar 4 onwards)
- Use of mutes (bar 2)
- Pizzicato (bar 7)
- The frequent separation of cello and double bass (e.g. bar 12)
- Hard drum sticks (bar 64)
- Violin melody doubled by flute to highlight the *idée fixe* (bar 71)
- The 'dry' rustling string support at the end of phrases here (bars 78–79)
- Restrained use of orchestral tutti effects, the first of which only occurs at bar 409
- At this point Berlioz divides the violin parts
- Measured tremolo (repeated quavers) at bar 461.

Texture

Textures are predominantly homophonic with occasional variations:

- Melody dominated homophony at bars 3–16
- Homorhythm (chords) at bars 511–525
- 'Layered', e.g. bar 48 onwards, with pedal in cellos and basses, triplet chords in flutes and clarinets, melody in horn and ornamental broken chords in violin I
- Largely monophonic announcement of *idée fixe* (bar 71)
- Melody frequently found in bass instruments, e.g. bars 166 onwards
- Octave woodwinds answered by octave strings (bars 191–197)
- The highly original streams of parallel first inversion chords in strings overlaid with long held woodwind and horn notes (bar 198 onwards)
- Broken chord accompaniment in low strings at bar 285 onwards
- Heterophony at bar 410 with violin line embroidering the *idée fixe* in violas, cornets and upper winds
- 'Dummy' imitations from bar 451, with close, overlapping appearances of the *idée fixe* in various instruments, but not to the extent that a genuine counterpoint is created.

Dynamics

Berlioz covers a dynamic range from *ppp* to *ff*.

Notice the extent to which he allocates different dynamics at the same point, e.g. the timpani *pp* at bar 511 in contrast to the *ppp* in the rest of the orchestra, this being the point at which the orchestra is directed to play as quietly as possible (*Tout l'orchestre aussi doux que possible*).

Tempo, metre and rhythm

- A slow introduction (Largo) is followed by the much faster Allegro agitato e appassionato assai (from bar 64) for the main part of the movement
- There are frequent variations in tempo, e.g. animez (bar 94) and retenu (bar 100)
- Metre at the start is simple quadruple (common time), changing to 'cut common' ($\frac{2}{2}$) from bar 64
- Notably varied rhythmic values are used, producing considerable fluidity:
  - Triplets at the opening
  - Dotted rhythms from bar 3
  - Sextuplets (plus vite) at bar 17, creating the impression of rapidity

- Cross rhythms, e.g. demisemiquavers in violas at bar 29 combined with sextuplet semiquavers in flute and clarinet while the theme from bar 3 in $\frac{4}{4}$ is heard
- Interpolation of quaver rests at bar 40 creates sighing effect
- Syncopation occurs frequently, e.g. bar 42 and bar 411
- Longer note lengths in *idée fixe* (see bar 72) and the closing 'Religiosamente'
- Anacrustic start to first phrases of *idée fixe*
- In marked contrast to the generally fluid approach is the passage of hard-driven, mechanical sounding crotchets from bar 198
- The prolonged general pause of three bars at bar 229
- The frequent use of patterns of two quavers followed by a crotchet rest.

Melody

Berlioz's lyric gifts are clear in this movement with melodic lines that unfold easily, often with asymmetrical phrasing. The first theme (bar 3), the melody taken from *Estelle et Némorin*, highlights many aspects of his style:

Bars 3–16

- Notice the differing phrase lengths
- The fluctuations between stepwise movement and leaps (variously minor 6th, perfect 4th, octave and 3rds)
- Fluidity underlined by frequent rests and pauses

- Appoggiaturas
- The extremely detailed dynamics marks.

The *idée fixe* itself, extracted from *Herminie*, shows many of the same characteristics in an even more pronounced form:

Bars 71–111

- Notice again the irregular phrase-lengths, bracketed on this example, of 8, 7, 4, 4, 4, 5, 2 and 6 (which could be subdivided into overlapping 1½ + 5) bars
- Contrasts of broken chord figures and step movement
- Use of rising sequence to build a climax

- Chromaticism
- Fluctuations in tempo
- The fact that significant portions of this theme are unaccompanied.

Much of the melodic writing is related to the *idée fixe*. The relatively brief second subject is a variant of the opening of the first subject:

Bars 150–154

Later in the movement a new line, heard in counterpoint to fragments of the *idée fixe*, appears on oboe:

Bars 358–367

Harmony

- Functional harmony, with a strong drive to cadences:
  - Imperfect at bar 10
  - Perfect at bars 71–72
  - Unusual III – I progression marking the end of the main allegro at bars 490–491
  - Plagal, both inverted (bars 511–513) and root position (bars 519–521)
- Pedals, the most intriguing of which is the A♭ from bars 46–59, supporting variously:
  - Diminished 7th (bar 46)
  - D♭ chord (bar 49)
  - E major, with the A♭ regarded as the enharmonic G♯, though the notation of the pedal remains unchanged (bar 53)
  - C♯ minor (bar 55)
  - G♯ minor (bar 57)
  - Diminished 7th again (bar 59)

- Besides the diminished 7th (see also bar 3), Berlioz uses 7ths and 9ths freely: see bar 10, where the dissonance is further intensified by the suspended C (11th)
- A further very striking harmonic effect is the stream of first inversions chords, starting in bar 198, moving chromatically.

Tonality and structure

- Slow introduction in a loose ternary form with extension
- Link
- An allegro which at first seems to suggest sonata form (see Clara Schumann's Piano Trio for an example of a traditional sonata form movement)
- The 'exposition' (bars 71–166) is repeated, and there is a modulation from tonic to dominant
- However, the basic scheme is subjected to numerous ingenious modifications and latterly evolves freely to such an extent that it is not possible to locate a conventional recapitulation.

Slow Introduction (Largo)		
Bars 1–2	Introduction	C minor
Bars 3–16	Theme from *Estelle et Némorin*	C minor
Bars 17–27	plus vite	C major → E♭
Bars 28–45	Theme from *Estelle et Némorin* extended	E♭ → C minor
Bars 46–63	Extension, over A♭ pedal to bar 59 New melodic material combined with triplets from Introduction	C minor (passing through D♭, A♭, E major, C♯ minor, G♯ minor)
Link		
Bars 64–71	Allegro agitato e appassionato assai	C major

Allegro		
Bars 71–111	Theme A: *Idée fixe* (from *Herminie*)	C
Bars 111–149	A extended, merging with transition	
Bars 150–166	Theme B: second subject based on A	G
Bars 166–231	Developmental section, with references to both A (bar 166, bass) and B (bar 191)	
Bars 232–278	Full statement of A	G
Bars 278–311	Further development	
Bars 311–329	B in quasi-fugal statement	C
Bars 329–410	Development and extension, involving new oboe theme (see example above of bars 358–367)	
Bars 410–491	Climax: tutti statement of A, followed by further working out	C
Bars 491–525	Coda, with pace slackening to 'Religiosamente'	C

FURTHER LISTENING

Investigate any programmatic symphonic music of the 19th and 20th centuries, e.g.

- **Beethoven, Symphony No. 6, *The Pastoral***
- **Liszt, *The Faust Symphony***
- **Richard Strauss, *Ein Heldenleben***
- **Shostakovich, Symphonies No. 11 (The Year 1905) and No. 12 (The Year 1917).**

AREA OF STUDY 3:

Music for film

'The Duchess' (Opening and End titles), 'Mistake of Your Life', 'Six Years Later' and 'Never See Your Children Again', from *The Duchess* (2008) (Rachel Portman)

Context

- *The Duchess* was released in 2008 and is based on the life of Georgina Cavendish, Duchess of Devonshire (1757–1806), her unhappy marriage, and affair with Charles Grey, 2nd Earl Grey
- The score is by Rachel Portman (b. 1960); her other film scores include *Chocolat* (2000) and *The Manchurian Candidate* (2004)
- Portman's scores avoid electronic and synthesised sound effects
- The score of *The Duchess* is made up of 18 cues, two of which are taken directly from classical sources (Beethoven's German Dance No. 10 and the Adagio from Haydn's String Quartet, Op. 1, No. 3)
- Classical pastiche is avoided in the cues, which Portman composed, in favour of a generally delicate underscore
- Two of the prescribed cues ('Mistake of Your Life' and 'Never See Your Children Again') effectively help to create a bleaker mood.

Notation

- The cues are notated in the form of orchestral short scores. The music is compressed for the most part on to two staves at a time with instrumentation indicated as required
- Tempo is indicated by metronome marks with occasional use of Italian terms
- Instrument names are given in English, although some Italian terminology is employed (tacet, tutti)
- Traditional dynamics marks are used.

Sonority

- Portman uses a relatively small orchestra, consisting of strings, woodwind, horns, harp and timpani

- Instruments are treated in a conventional manner, with some use of string pizzicato (e.g. 'Six Years Later')
- A violin solo can be heard in the first cue ('The Duchess' (Opening), bar 17)
- Effective use is made of solo timpani in 'Mistake of Your Life'.

Texture

- Melody-dominated homophony is used in all the prescribed cues, but notice:
  - Pedal in the Opening (bars 17–36)
  - Dominant pedal with timpani rhythm in 'Mistake of Your Life'
  - Waltz patterns in 'Six Years Later'
  - Thinning out of texture at the close of 'Six Years Later'.

Tempo, metre and rhythm

Tempo

- Moderately fast for the Opening and End Titles
- Brisk waltz time for 'Six Years Later'
- Slow for 'Mistake of Your Life' and 'Never See Your Children Again'

Metre

- Quadruple for Opening and End Titles, and second part of 'Six Years Later'
- Compound duple ($\frac{6}{8}$) for first part of 'Six Years Later' with two bars of triple-time waltz for each $\frac{6}{8}$ bar
- Triple time for 'Mistake of Your Life' and 'Never See Your Children Again'

Rhythm

- Continuous quavers in both fast and slow movements
- Syncopation in the Opening (see accompaniment in bar 1 and melody in bar 10)
- Occasional triplets in the Opening (e.g. bar 22)
- Ominous timpani pattern in both 'Mistake of Your Life' (shown below) and 'Never See Your Children Again'

- Long sustained notes in 'Never See Your Children Again'.

Melody

- There is some use of modality, e.g. the melody of the Opening is in D major, but there are mixolydian inflections, e.g. the C♮ in bar 7
- In all cues, there is frequent step movement, sometimes interspersed with leaps of 3rd, 4th, 6th (e.g. in the Opening)
- Other features include:
  - Appoggiaturas (e.g. bar 18 of the Opening)
  - Auxiliary notes (e.g. bars 2 and 35 of the Opening)
  - Sequential repetition (e.g. 'Mistake of Your Life', bar 27, where the preceding eight-bar phrase in G minor is repeated a tone higher in A minor)
  - Expressive minor 6ths (e.g. 'Mistake of your life', piano bars 35–38):

  - Melody formed from broken chords, in bars 3–6 of 'Six Years Later':

Harmony

- Harmony is broadly functional with perfect cadences (e.g. the Opening, bars 13–16)
- Harmonic rhythm (i.e. rate of chord change) is generally slow
- Modal elements are evident, with the frequent use of a 'modal' dominant chord, i.e. where the leading note is lowered a semitone so that in place of an A major chord, an A minor chord is used in the Opening and End Titles, while in 'Mistake of Your Life', a D minor chord replaces D major in the key of G minor
- Other devices include:
  - Use of unprepared and unresolved 7ths, e.g. the Opening, bar 11
  - Pedal points, e.g. tonic (the Opening, bars 17–36) and dominant ('Mistake of your life', bars 1–18)
  - Internal pedal ('Never See Your Children Again', bars 7–25)
  - Harmonic sequences ('Mistake of Your Life', bars 19–34)
  - Open 5th chords ('Mistake of Your Life', bar 73)
  - Unstable second inversion for final cadence ('Mistake of Your Life', bars 81–82)
  - Augmented triad ('Six Years Later', bars 25 and 27)

- Diminished triad (bars 34–37) and unprepared dissonances (e.g. added E against the opening pedal D) in 'Never See Your Children Again'
- Variation of basic vocabulary in 'End Titles' through the addition of chords of F major, G major (first inversion) and E min7.

Tonality

- Tonality of the Opening, 'Six Years Later' and End Titles is D mixolydian. The C♯, which would have occurred in a major scale, is replaced with a C♮. These three cues have no modulation
- The key of 'Mistake of Your Life' is G minor, with both modal and ordinary 'functional' dominant chords
- In 'Mistake of Your Life', there are brief excursions to A minor
- 'Never See Your Children Again' is in a non-functional D minor.

Structure

- This score is less concerned with matching specific images to the course of the music than the creation of a more generally expressive underscore. Consequently there are clear traces of formal musical organisation and symmetry, as well as the reprising of large parts of already announced material, e.g. the repetitions of music from the Opening in the second section of 'Six years later' and the modified repetitions in the End Titles.
- The Opening consists of three separate themes heard one after another and without development:

Bars 1–16

Bars 35–43: motif **X** is also extended in the End Titles

- 'Mistake of Your Life' consists of an introduction followed by two themes heard in alternation. These themes share a resemblance with motifs from the Opening. (Compare bars 17–34 on page 67 with the first theme of this cue):

- 'Six Years Later' is in two sections: first a 'waltz', which in harmonic content (tonic–'modal' dominant) relates to the Opening; and secondly a substantial reprise of music from the Opening.

- 'Never See Your Children Again' is more atmospheric, and is through-composed

- 'End titles' largely follows the course of the Opening, although one motif in particular (marked **x** on page 67) is subjected to more development, and the harmonic vocabulary is expanded to take in additional chords.

Main theme ('Birth of a Penguin Part II'), 'Birth of a Penguin Part 1', 'Rise and Fall from Grace' and 'Batman vs the Circus', from *Batman Returns* (1992) (Danny Elfman)

Context

- The *Batman* films are fantasies based on the comic-book character Batman, and his encounters with ingenious criminals, in this case the Penguin and Catwoman

- *Batman Returns* was directed by Tim Burton, and is a sequel to his *Batman* (1989)

- The score was provided by Danny Elfman (b.1953), composer of incidental music for film and TV, perhaps most famously for *The Simpsons*

- The score is popular and direct in style, with vivid, grand orchestral effects

- Much of the orchestration was undertaken by Steve Bartek, aided by Mark McKenzie

- Elfman uses a leitmotif system, with clearly defined themes for each character.

The term Leitmotif was first used in connection with the operas of Wagner, where motifs were used to represent the characters and also objects (e.g. swords) and concepts (e.g. love, grief). In the course of his operas such motifs were subjected to development and transformation as the changing situation demanded, and a similar process occurs in Elfman's score.

Notation

- The cues are notated in the form of orchestral short scores. The music is compressed onto varying numbers of staves, ranging from two or three up to nine in 'Batman vs the Circus', with instrumentation and vocal parts indicated as required.

'Cue' is the term used to indicate the music used for a particular point or scene in the film.

Sonority

Elfman draws on a full symphony orchestra, and the following additional instruments:

- Organ
- A children's choir
- Synthesiser
- Celeste
- Piano
- Accordion
- Large percussion section, including xylophone, marimba, temple blocks, sleighbells, tam-tam, cymbals

Colouristic effects include:

- Strings – tremolandi, pizzicato, glissandi
- Woodwinds – flutter-tongue (flute); wide vibrato (oboe)
- Brass – use of mutes, horn glissando
- Choir – vocalisation.

Texture

Textures are generally homophonic:

- Chordal ('Birth of a Penguin Part I', bar 14)
- Melody-dominated homophony ('Birth of a Penguin Part II', bar 27 onwards – this is the Batman motif)
- Layered ostinati (opening of 'Birth of a Penguin Part II')
- Octaves ('Birth of a Penguin Part I', bars 22–25)
- High pitch string clusters ('The Rise and Fall from Grace', bars 7–8)
- Waltz rhythm with sustained octaves in bass ('Rise and Fall', bars 20–25)
- Pedal ('Birth of a Penguin Part II', bars 85–92).

Tempo, metres and rhythm

Tempo

- Indicated by metronome marks
- Most of the cues are moderate in pace, though 'Batman vs the Circus' moves from slow to very fast.

Metre

- There are occasional changes of time signature, e.g. one bar of $\frac{3}{8}$ at bar 13 of 'Birth of a Penguin Part I', and the insertion of the waltz episode (bars 20–25) within a mainly quadruple time context for 'Rise and Fall from Grace'.

Rhythm

- Notable **rhythmic** features include:
  - Pounding triplets in the Batman theme and its accompaniment ('Birth of a Penguin Part II', bar 25 onwards)
  - Loose augmentations, e.g. bar 65 of 'Birth of a Penguin Part II'
  - Almost constant quavers in 'Batman vs the Circus'.

Melody

- The two most important leitmotifs are:
  - The Batman motif and its variants:

Birth of a Penguin Part I, bar 1

Birth of a Penguin Part II, bar 27

- Motifs associated with the Penguin, first of which is a four-note idea:

Birth of a Penguin Part I, bar 3

- The second motif appears briefly in the course of the opening cue, but can be heard most clearly in 'Rise and Fall from Grace'

Rise and Fall from Grace, bars 8–11

- Fragmentary melodic lines occur in 'Batman vs the Circus' (oboe at bars 57–58, the fairground steam organ at bars 62–63)
- The first of the Penguin motifs occurs as part of a quaver 'moto perpetuo' in 'Batman vs the Circus', bars 26–27. Notice the first of each four-quaver group:

Batman versus the Circus, bars 26–27

Harmony

- Functional language, with frequent cadences
- Tonic pedals (e.g. 'Birth of a Penguin Part II', bars 1–8)
- Diminished triads (e.g. 'Birth of a Penguin Part I', bar 34³)
- Diminished 7th ('Birth of a Penguin Part I', bar 37²)
- Augmented triad ('Rise and Fall from Grace', bar 51)
- False relations ('Birth of a Penguin Part II', bars 93–96)
- Added 6th chords ('Batman vs the Circus', bar 5)
- Neapolitan harmony ('Rise and Fall from Grace', bar 45)
- Whole-tone chords ('Rise and Fall from Grace', bars 50–52).

Structure and tonality

- All the prescribed cues are through-composed, drawing on the various leitmotifs, as and when the film action requires
- Keys are clearly defined by cadences and sometimes by pedals
- Tonality is not structurally significant. For example, 'Birth of a Penguin Part I' opens in B♭ minor and closes in D minor, 'Birth of a Penguin Part II' continues in D minor and finishes in C♯ minor
- 'Batman versus the Circus' opens in B minor and closes in E minor
- 'Rise and Fall from Grace' is the only one of the prescribed cues to remain anchored to a single tonality (C minor – C major)
- Key changes are often sudden, e.g. 'Birth of a Penguin Part I' moves from F minor (bars 3–6), A minor (bars 7–10) and then to G minor (bars 11–13)
- Key changes sometimes involve keys unrelated to one another, e.g. 'Birth of a Penguin Part I', bars 26–31 in D minor to bars 32–33 in F♯ minor and then bars 34–37 in G minor
- Sense of key is occasionally weakened by use of whole-tone structures, e.g. bars 50–52 in 'Rise and Fall from Grace'.

'Prelude', 'The City', 'Marion', 'The Murder' (Shower Scene), 'The Toys', 'The Cellar', 'Discovery', 'Finale' from *Psycho* (Bernard Herrmann)

Context

- Bernard Herrmann (1911–1975) trained at New York University and the Juilliard School
- He developed his skills as a writer of background music at CBS where he worked in Radio Theatre
- Notable film scores include:
  - *Citizen Kane* (1940) directed by Orson Wells
  - *Vertigo* (1958), *North by North West* (1959) and *Psycho* (1960) for Alfred Hitchcock
  - *Fahrenheit 451* (1966) for Truffaut
  - *Taxi Driver* (1976) for Martin Scorsese
- Herrmann orchestrated his own works
- His style is marked by:
  - A preference for motifs and ostinati over extended lyrical lines
  - Extreme dissonance
  - Chromaticism.

Psycho

- *Psycho* was released in 1960
- It was based on Robert Bloch's novel of the same name, published in 1959, with a screenplay by Joseph Stefano
- This celebrated horror film was largely set in a Gothic-style motel: the set was modelled on Edward Hopper's painting, *The House by the Railroad* (1925)
- It was made on a low budget in black and white, but enjoyed enormous success and critical acclaim
- Herrmann's score contributed much to the success of the film, Hitchcock himself commenting '33% of the effect of *Psycho* was due to the music'.

Notation

Music for 'Prelude', 'The City', 'The Murder', 'The Toys' and 'The Cellar' are notated in full score with each instrument allotted its own stave. Reduced scores, in which some staves contain combinations of different parts, are used in the remainder. Traditional (i.e. Italian) dynamics, tempo marks and other indications are employed.

Sonority

- Unusually, the entire film score is orchestrated for strings only, rather than full symphony orchestra or the jazz band initially suggested by Hitchcock
- The forces required were 14 first violins, 12 seconds, 10 violas, 8 cellos and 6 double basses
- Furthermore, the strings were muted throughout except for the shower scene
- To intensify the harsh sound in the shower scene, microphones were placed close to the instruments
- Numerous performing techniques are used for variety and expressive force:
  - Double stopped chords ('Prelude')
  - Repeated down bows ('Prelude' and shower scene)
  - Combinations of arco and pizzicato ('Prelude' and shower scene)
  - Glissandi (shower scene)
  - Tremolandi (on divisi strings) ('The Cellar')
  - Sul ponticello ('The Cellar')
  - Relatively high lines ('Finale').

Texture

Many contrasting textures are employed:

- Chords ('Prelude', bars 1 and 21)
- Ostinati and pedals supporting short motifs ('Prelude', bar 5)
- Melody with tremolandi and chordal accompaniment ('Prelude', bar 37)
- Varying densities:
  - Two-part ('Finale', bars 1–9)
  - Three-part ('Marion', bars 1–9)
  - Eight-part with divisi in all four sections except double bass ('The City', bar 1)
  - Four-part divisi in both violin I and II ('The Toys')
- Octaves ('The Cellar', bars 1–4)
- Imitative entries in 'The Cellar' from bar 5, creating a sort of fugal exposition
- Homorhythmic chords ('Discovery', bars 1–18)
- Free counterpoint ('Finale', bars 3–17).

Dynamics

Herrmann covers a full range of dynamics from *ppp* in 'The Toys' to unmuted *sffz* at the opening of the shower scene.

Tempo, metre and rhythm

The cues selected for study are widely contrasted in terms of tempo, metre and rhythm:

- Fast-paced music can be found in 'The Prelude' (Allegro (molto agitato)), 'The Cellar' (Allegro molto) and 'Discovery' (Allegro feroce)
- Duple time is used in the above movements, although 'Discovery' closes with extremely fast triple time music
- The shower scene is a moderately paced, but relentless triple time movement
- 'The City', 'Marion', and the 'The Toys' are in a much slower quadruple time, while the slow 'Finale' music alternates between quadruple and triple time
- Other notable features include:
  - Constant, hard-driven quavers ('Prelude' and 'The Cellar')
  - Triplets ('Prelude')
  - Dotted rhythms ('Prelude')
  - Distinctive rhythmic pattern at the opening of 'Prelude' which is frequently repeated
  - Steadily moving crotchets ('The City')
  - Syncopation ('Marion', throughout, 'Discovery', bars 1–2 and 'Finale', viola at bars 12–14)
  - Cross-rhythms ('Discovery', bar 19 with semiquavers against triplet crotchets).

Melody and motifs

In general, Herrmann avoided leitmotifs, i.e. motifs which appear throughout the entire film score, preferring to compose individual material for each cue. However, the opening chord reappears intermittently.

- 'The Prelude' is based on three short motifs and one more extended melody
  - The first is less melodic than harmonic and rhythmic:

'Prelude', bars 1–3

- Motif 2 is a triplet figure, supported by semitonal ostinato. Its second bar is composed of the same pitches, now in even quavers:

'Prelude', bars 5–6

- Motif 3 is marked by dotted rhythms and sequential repetition:

'Prelude', bars 21–22

- The Prelude's remaining thematic element is a melodic line which appears three times. It contrasts with the motifs because:
  - It is conjunct
  - It consists of three four-bar phrases:

'Prelude', bars 37–48

- 'The City' consists of four three-bar phrases (two bars plus one bar), the opening descent answered by a loose inversion in the second. A similar pattern is used in the remaining two phrases

- The melody of 'Marion' is in diatonic C major and is marked by:
  - Descending sequence of a three-note figure
  - Perfect 5ths:

'Marion', bars 1–4

- The shower scene has no discernible melody
- 'The Toys' is a very brief cue and is diatonic, with
  - A descending conjunct line
  - Three three-bar phrases
- 'The Cellar' is markedly more chromatic throughout:
  - The pitch outline in bars 1–4 (D–A–A♭) anticipates the chromaticism of the fugal subject at bar 5
  - The subject initially moves by semitonal step
  - Latterly it expands intervallically to embrace major and minor 3rds, diminished 5th and minor 6th

'The Cellar', Introduction and opening subject

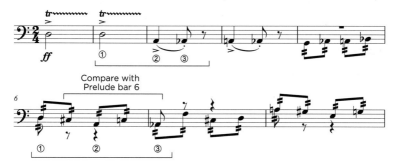

- 'Discovery' is again highly chromatic with prominent semitones, tritones and perfect 4ths
  - It relates to 'The Cellar' as its first three notes are a retrograde of the opening motif of 'The Cellar'
  - Typical melodic devices include:
    - Sequential repetition
    - Octave shifts

- The 'Finale' is notable for:
  - Chromaticism
  - Angular intervals, especially augmented 4ths and diminished 5ths
  - A three-note motif (F–E♭–D) quoted from Herrmann's own Sinfonietta for Strings, as well as his cantata *Moby Dick*:

'Finale', bars 17–19

Harmony

Herrmann's harmonic writing in this film score is non-functional in that he avoids cadential harmony. In general, it is notable for its high dissonance levels and chromaticism. Even the less ferocious movements avoid consonance, tending to be characterised by a more diatonic approach.

Typical devices are:

- 'Signature' chord of B♭ minor plus 7th (see first example above)
- Use of pedal points, e.g. 'Prelude', bars 5–20, and throughout 'The Toys'
- 'Higher' dissonances, e.g. 13th chords ('Prelude', bar 21) and characteristic minor 9th closing 'The Finale'
- Simultaneous false relation, e.g. the G and G♯ in 'Prelude', bar 21
- Diminished 7th ('The City', bar 1, where the chord is widely spaced)
- Half-diminished 7ths ('The City', bars 1–2):

'The City', bar 1

- Added 6th chords, e.g. A minor with F♯ in 'The City', bar 3
- Suspensions, e.g. 'Marion', in bar 2 between outer parts
- Extreme dissonance formed by major 7ths and diminished octaves (e.g. the shower scene, bars 1–8)

- Tritone chord (shower scene, bars 35–37)

- Parallel 7ths ('The Toys', bar 3 onwards)

- Augmented triad ('The Cellar', bar 68 to the end, latterly combined with a diminished triad)

- Verticalisations of melodic content to form chords, an idea taken from serial (12-tone) music, e.g. 'Discovery', bar 1, where the first chord contains all the notes of the melody

- Chromatically moving parallel dissonant chords, 'Discovery', bar 26 onwards.

Structure and tonality

- In the absence of cadential harmony, Herrmann relies on pedals, ostinati and 'signature' or characteristic recurring chords, e.g. the opening B♭ 7th of 'The Prelude' or concluding 9th of 'The Finale'

- In some cues, there are surviving traces of 'key', e.g. the unrealised A minor at the close of 'The City' and the phrygian mode of 'The Toys' (i.e. a 'white-note' scale based on E) used throughout

- Some of the cues are so brief that it is only possible to speak of an underlying phrase-structure:

  - 'The City': five three-bar phrases plus concluding chord

  - 'Marion': four sets of four bars with additional concluding dissonance (an inconclusive expanded dominant within C major)

  - 'The Toys': three three-bar phrases, with two-bar introduction and concluding bar

- The (slightly) more extended cues include:

  - The shower scene, which in spite of the prominence of particular notes, is virtually non-tonal and consists of two eight-bar sections, the second varied by use of glissandi. A 21-bar coda (death of Marion) is built on two chords:

'The Murder', bars 17–18

  - 'Discovery' is atonal and through-composed, with component bars reappearing in contrasting combinations, e.g. bars 8–9 are composed of bar 1 followed by bar 6

- 'Finale' is also through-composed and atonal, with a final unresolved dissonance

- 'The Prelude' is built on the alternation of the three motifs and melody given above, held together by driving ostinato, pedal points and a strong focus on the opening B♭ minor harmony. There are constant elaborations and variations of the basic material, and a striking unrelated D♮ at the close which has an alienating effect

- 'The Cellar' could be likened to a short introduction and fugue, though it should be stressed that Herrmann does not follow traditional fugal procedures (see Vivaldi):

    - Bars 1–4 form the introduction

    - Bar 5 sees the fugue subject (on G), split between cello and double bass

    - Subsequent entries begin on G (as opposed to the traditional dominant)

    - Rhythmic dislocations of the subject occur at bars 32 and 40.

FURTHER LISTENING

Many aspects of Herrmann's writing in *Psycho* suggest the influence of Bartók, so it would be useful to listen to his *Music for Strings, Percussion and Celesta* and String Quartets No. 4 and No. 5.

It would also be worth listening to and/or viewing Herrmann's scores for *Vertigo* (1958) and *North by North West* (1959).

AREA OF STUDY 4:
Popular music and jazz

'Lady Day and (John Coltrane)', 'Inner State (of Mind)' and 'Love and Affection', from *Back in the Day* (2000) (Courtney Pine)

Context

- Courtney Pine (b.1964) is a contemporary jazz musician, whose style blends soul, rhythm and blues, reggae, and hip hop with traditional elements

- He is a virtuoso saxophonist, who also performs on flute, bass clarinet and keyboards

- *Back in the Day* (issued in 2000) was Pine's eighth album, one which he produced himself

- Three of the album's 15 tracks are prescribed for study, and two of these are cover versions: 'Lady Day and (John Coltrane)' by Gil Scott-Heron (1971) and 'Love and affection' by Joan Armatrading (1976).

Notation

- The Anthology shows a short score with piano, vocal, and chord symbols with guitar tab above the stave. Other instrumental parts are notated on an additional stave, as required

- Cross-heads are used to indicate the rhythms in the rap sections as well as multiphonics and key-click effects

- Dynamics are shown in a traditional manner

- Tempo is given as beats per minute

- Occasionally, other effects are written into the score, e.g. vibrato, bar 39.

Sonority

There is a considerable contrast of instruments used between the three songs:

- 'Lady Day and (John Coltrane)' is scored for vocals, piano, guitars and saxophone
- 'Inner State (of Mind)' draws on the so-called 'jazz horn' grouping, which confusingly does not include horns but instead saxophone, trumpet and trombone. Other resources include vocals, rap and guitars
- 'Love and affection' includes vocal, bvox, guitar, bass clarinet, tenor sax and strings.

Notice the following features:

- Distortions and random background sounds at start of 'Inner State (of Mind)'
- Dubbed voices in 'Inner State (of Mind)' and 'Lady Day and (John Coltrane)'
- Use of what the CD sleeve notes call a 'drum programme' in 'Inner State (of Mind)' and 'Lady Day and (John Coltrane)'
- Extended performance techniques (multiphonics and key clicks) in 'Lady Day and (John Coltrane)'
- Variation of vocal timbres in 'Love and affection'.

Texture

The predominant texture is homophony or melody-dominated homophony. See table below for locations of various features:

Texture	'Inner State (of Mind)'	'Lady Day and (John Coltrane)'	'Love and affection'
Homophonic	Voices (bar 1) Horns and sax (bars 70–71)	Close harmony (bar 21)	
Melody-dominated homophony	e.g. bars 2–9 (sax and piano)	Bar 1 onwards	Bars 1–12
Rap with accompaniment	e.g. bars 21–35		

Broken chords	Bars 80–87 (RH piano)		
Riff	e.g. bars 94–115	e.g. bars 5–12	e.g. bars 22 onwards
Free counterpoint			Bars 84–94

Tempo, metre and rhythm

- 'Inner State (of Mind)' is in a brisk quadruple metre throughout
- 'Lady Day and (John Coltrane)' moves from fast quadruple to a slower rubato section at the close
- 'Love and Affection' opens with a rubato quadruple time passage, before moving into an upbeat strict tempo.

Rhythmic features are located in the table below. (There are many other instances of some of these, which you might find it helpful to write in):

Rhythmic features	'Inner state (of mind)'	'Lady Day and (John Coltrane)'	'Love and affection'
Syncopation	e.g. bars 2 and 3		
Dotted rhythm	Bar 11	Bar 81	
Scotch snap	Bar 75	Bar 31	
Triplets		Bar 126	Bar 25
Irregular groupings	Bar 97		Bar 31

Long sustained notes	Bars 46–48	
Off-beat chords		Bars 13–14
Cross-rhythms		Bar 12 ('really laugh')

Melody

The prescribed songs are typically characterised by:

- Pentatonicism (e.g. 'Inner State (of Mind)', bars 1–2; 'Love and Affection' strings motif uses minor pentatonic scale, bars 84–85)
- Blue notes (e.g. 'Inner State (of Mind)', bar 2, G♭; 'Lady Day and (John Coltrane), bar 23, G♭)
- Chromaticism (e.g. 'Inner State (of Mind)', bar 100, note the ornamented chromatic descent C–B–B♭–A; 'Lady Day', bar 75; 'Love and Affection', bass clarinet, bars 30–32).

Other noteworthy features include:

- Borrowing of melody from Gershwin's 'Summertime' from *Porgy and Bess* in 'Inner State (of Mind)'
- Scat singing ('Inner State (of Mind)', bars 52–53)
- Melismas ('Love and Affection', bar 47)
- Conjunct lines ('Love and Affection', bars 16–19)
- Narrow-range lines ('Lady Day and (John Coltrane)', bars 5–7)
- Repetition of short figures ('Inner state (of Mind), bar 99)
- Frequent ornamentation, e.g. in 'Lady Day and (John Coltrane)':
  - Acciaccaturas (bar 8)
  - Controlled vibrato (bar 39)
  - Bending of notes (bar 45)
  - Fall-offs (bar 50)
  - Sliding up to pitch (bar 52)
  - Glissandos (bar 55).

Harmony

- 12-bar blues ('Lady Day and (John Coltrane)')
- 7th chords ('Lady Day and (John Coltrane)', bar 21)
- 7ths are sometimes laced with ♮9ths, which produce false relations ('Lady Day and (John Coltrane)', bar 1)
- 9th chords ('Lady Day and (John Coltrane)', bar 47)
- 13th chords ('Lady Day and (John Coltrane)', bar 81)
- Some quartal harmony ('Inner State (of Mind)', bars 70–71)
- False relations ('Inner State (of Mind)', bar 18)
- Half-diminished chords ('Inner state (of Mind)', bar 53³)
- Augmented chord ('Lady Day and (John Coltrane)', bar 119)
- Parallel harmony ('Lady Day and (John Coltrane)', parallel 7th chords, bar 65)
- Change of harmonic rhythm, i.e. rate of chord changes per bar (final section of 'Lady Day and (John Coltrane)', from bar 119)
- Use of basic (non-extended) chords (opening of 'Love and Affection')
- Primary chords ('Love and Affection', bar 22 onwards)
- Chromatic side-stepping ('Love and Affection', bar 62 onwards).

Tonality and structure

- 'Inner State (of Mind)' is in C minor with a modal (two flat) key signature. Its structure is freely evolving, with the recurring 'Inner State' motif, instrumentals and alternating verse (supported by riff) and rap sections
- 'Lady Day and (John Coltrane)' is also in C minor. It is a modified 12-bar blues with introduction and extended coda
- 'Love and Affection' opens in C♯ minor but continues in E major. Its freely evolving structure starts with an introduction before moving into a riff-based song with a prominent refrain.

'Cloudbusting', 'And Dream of Sheep' and 'Under Ice' from *Hounds of Love* (Kate Bush)

Context

- Kate Bush (b.1958) is a performer and composer of progressive rock
- Her music sometimes contains Irish elements, stemming from her family connections
- The album *Hounds of Love* was released in 1985 and draws on vocals, piano (played by Bush), balalaika, string sextet, bouzouki and uilleann pipes
- The album was produced by Bush in her own studio
- In part, it could be classed as a concept album: the first side of the original vinyl recording consists of five progressive rock songs; the second side, 'The Ninth Wave', was based very loosely on Tennyson's poetic work *Idylls of the King*
- 'Cloudbusting' is the last of the progressive rock songs on side one of the vinyl. It is based on incidents in the life and career of the psychologist Wilhelm Reich
- The first two songs from the original side two, 'And Dream of Sheep' and 'Under Ice', depict the thoughts of a drowning girl.

'Cloudbusting' is based on Bush's reading of Peter Reich's *A Book of Dreams*, and in particular the imprisonment and death of psychoanalyst Wilhelm Reich (1897–1957) in the USA.

Notation

In the Anthology, staff notation is used with guitar chords indicated above the system. Speeds are indicated in beats per minute, but variations in tempo and dynamic signs are given in a traditional form. Each song uses a different type of layout, as follows:

- 'Cloudbusting' is a full score. The string sextet parts are mainly printed on two staves, but occasionally the more active violin parts are allotted a separate stave. Parts for voice, backing vocals, three keyboards, balalaika and percussion are scored separately
- 'And Dream of Sheep' is notated for voice and piano, with additional staves introduced as required for bouzouki and whistles
- 'Under Ice' is a short score, with parts indicated as required on three or four staves.

Sonority

A wide range of resources and timbres are employed in the three prescribed works:

- Though vocals, Fairlight CMI (Computer Musical Instrument, i.e. synthesiser) and drums play a major role in 'Cloudbusting', the most distinctive timbre is the string sextet (calling to mind 'Eleanor Rigby' by The Beatles). There are also occasional appearances of balalaika

- 'And Dream of Sheep' is the most conventional popular music timbre of the three songs, with voice and piano dominating. There are also additional parts for bouzouki (a plucked string instrument used in Greek and modern Irish music) and whistles. The sound is further intensified by the use of dubbed voices

- Unusual atmospheric timbres are created in 'Under Ice' through the use of synthesised strings and a low vocal tessitura.

Textures

Melody-dominated homophony predominates throughout, but notice particularly:

- Persistent detached chords for strings in 'Cloudbusting', as well as:
  - Fragmentary patterns on keyboard
  - Counter-melody in octaves in the violin
  - Expansion of texture with the three lowest strings and keyboard 3 providing sustained semibreves
- Broken-chord figures in 'And Dream of Sheep'
- The lean sound in 'Under Ice' is created by the fragmentary vocal line, supported by bass octaves and two-part synthesised string motifs, mainly in 4ths and 5ths; a soft synth pad sounds throughout.

Tempo, metre and rhythm

'Cloudbusting'

This song is in a moderate, rather mechanical strict time. The time signature is mainly quadruple, with occasional changes (to $\frac{6}{4}$ and $\frac{2}{4}$).

Rhythmic features include:

- Constant crotchet beat established at the start by the strings
- Steady, reinforcing crotchet drum-beats from bar 11
- Backbeat
- Mechanical patterns in the violin (see bar 3)

- Effective halt to the mechanical rhythms at key words, e.g. 'I won't forget' (bar 50)
- Semibreves in the lower parts (bar 95), combined with a strong rhythmic figure in the upper string parts.
- Longer note values in the violin counter-melody beginning in bar 34, and in the additional synthesised line at bar 65
- Syncopation, e.g. keyboard 2 (bar 69–70).

'Dream of Sheep'

This song uses a moderately slow quadruple metre with occasional changes of signature. Rubato, rits and fermata ⌢ are employed. Notice the use of dotted rhythm, triplets and Scotch snap.

'Under Ice'

In this song, the tempo speeds up from 65 beats per minute to 108 and then slows at the close. The metre is largely irregular, starting and ending in quadruple time but frequently alternating with triple time sections.

Other prominent rhythmic features include:

- A two quaver–crotchet pattern, first heard in strings and taken over in the voice part
- A two-note figure with longer second note (vocal part, bars 12–13, 'so white')
- The long-sustained synth pad, which enters in bar 2
- Scotch snaps (e.g. bar 27)
- Triplets (e.g. bar 50).

Melody

'Cloudbusting'

- Modal, based in C♯ aeolian minor with occasional focus on B major
- Lead vocal is a minor 10th, from G♯ below middle C to B above
- Word setting is predominantly syllabic, with very occasional slurred pairs
- Opens with leaps of 3rds, 4ths and 5ths, but then narrows in range
- Portamento
- Other melodic features include:
  - The violin's opening narrow-range motif, featuring some chromaticism
  - The violin's later counter-melody, with step-wise descent
  - An additional melody line in keyboard 2, starting at bar 65
  - Bvox vocalisation with leap of minor 7th (bar 111).

'And Dream of Sheep'

- E major
- Vocal range is a major 9th (B–C♯), though for the most part occupies the lower part of this span (B–G♯)
- Distinctive perfect 5ths in the opening phrase
- Repeated notes
- Word setting is mainly syllabic, with brief melismas at phrase-endings
- Repeated 3rds at 'If they find me racing…'.

'Under Ice'

- Vocal range is a minor 10th (A–C), with low notes favoured for the most part
- Characterised by a mainly step-wise two-pitch figure
- A more lyrical phrase occurs at 'The river has frozen over', with leaps of 4ths and a 5th
- Word-setting is mainly syllabic, with some slurred pairs
- Descending chromatic portamento at close.

Harmony

'Cloudbusting'

- The song's mechanical feel is intensified through the frequent use of a limited number of dissonant added-note chords (C♯m[7]–B major with added 9th – A major with added 9th and 6th, and the occasional G♯ minor chord with added 4th)
- All chords contain both B and C♯
- Harmonic rhythm is varied: e.g. at the opening the C♯ and B chords have two beats; whereas at bar 95, the chords are allotted four beats.

'And Dream of Sheep'

- Functional harmony in the key of E major
- Typical chords include I, IIb, V, VI[7], IV with added 9th
- Tonic pedal at 'If they find me racing…'
- A chord of perfect 4ths played on whistles at bar 41.

'Under Ice'

- Conventional chords avoided
- Bass hints at functional structure, with the tonic (A), submediant (F), mediant (C), and subdominant (D)
- The dominant (E) is avoided.

Tonality and structure

'Cloudbusting'

This song is in C♯ minor with no modulation. Broadly, the song follows a verse and chorus pattern with instrumentals:

Bars	Section
1–8	Verse
9–18	Bridge
18–33	Chorus
34–41	Verse
42–51	Bridge
51–68	Chorus
69–81	Instrumental, involving synthesised melody
81–98	Chorus
99–136	Instrumental and coda, featuring chorus material and Bvox

'And Dream of Sheep'

This song is in E major throughout, and is loosely strophic:

Bars	Section
1–15	Verse
15–19	Link 1
19–36	Verse
36–40	Link 2
40–53	Coda

'Under Ice'

The bass notes indicate clearly that this song is in A minor. The tonality is clouded at the end by the chromaticism and background electronic effects.

The song is through-composed, with alternating fragmentary melodic motifs:

Bars	Section
1–8	Introduction
8–13	Motif 1
14–18	Motif 2
19–24	Motif 1
24–29	Motif 2
30–39	Motif 1
40–45	Motif 2
46–58	Motif 1 and coda

'Eleanor Rigby', 'Here, There and Everywhere', 'I Want to Tell You', and 'Tomorrow Never Knows' from *Revolver* (The Beatles)

Context

- The music of the Beatles initially drew on rock-and-roll, blues and folk music
- *Revolver,* their seventh album, was released on 5 August 1966
- It was produced by George Martin and recorded and mixed by Geoff Emerick
- It marked a new departure as it was essentially studio-based and thus enabled the incorporation of experimental effects impossible in live performance:
  - Automatic double-tracking, i.e. use of two linked tape recorders to create a doubled track on one take, the second track being delayed a fraction of a second to give the impression that two parts were involved
  - Variable tape speeds, e.g. recording at a faster tempo than was eventually heard on the disc
  - Use of tape loops, i.e. cutting and splicing of tape to create a circle or loop which can be played continuously
  - Playing recorded sounds backwards ('backmasking')
  - Dubbed sound effects
- Other notable features included:
  - Use of such classical performance forces as the 'doubled' string quartet in 'Eleanor Rigby' and horn in 'For No One'
  - Indian influences, e.g. sitar and tabla in 'Love You Too' and sitar in 'Tomorrow Never Knows'
  - Increasingly free treatment of conventional popular music structures
  - Presence of 'psychedelic' elements arising from experimentation with LSD and resulting in increasingly colourful musical timbres
  - Wider range of subjects covered: of the four prescribed songs, only 'Here, There and Everywhere' is a conventional love-song.

Notation

- 'Eleanor Rigby': string quartet notation is used for the instruments with separate staves for violin I, violin II, viola and cello; the two backing vocal parts are notated on one stave, and the lead vocal on another

- 'Here, There and Everywhere' and 'I Want to Tell You' use staff notation for piano and vocals, with chord symbols above the stave for guitars
- 'Tomorrow Never Knows' initially has staves for voice, sitar, bass guitar (on two separate staves, one of them tab) and drums; verbal indications are given to indicate entries of the various loops
- Tempo indications are given in terms of numbers of beats per minute for all songs, except 'Tomorrow Never Knows' which has no marking
- Conventional dynamic indications are most detailed in 'Eleanor Rigby', but are limited in the remaining numbers.

'Eleanor Rigby'

This strikingly original song is concerned with loneliness and futility.

Sonority

- String group of eight performers, in effect a doubled string quartet
- George Martin arranged the string parts, influenced in part by Bernard Herrmann's score for *Psycho*
- Mechanical staccato figurations
- Performed non-vibrato, and recorded with microphones close to the instruments
- Vocal harmonies, with the line doubled a 3rd below at the opening, were provided by Lennon and Harrison
- McCartney sang the verses.

Texture

- The texture is predominantly homophonic
- Repeated staccato chords contrast with sustained notes in other parts, e.g. bar 19, with descending chromatic line in viola, and pedal in cello
- Texture is subsequently varied:
  - Rising scale in quavers in cello (bar 30)
  - Sustained, syncopated viola line, broadly a 6th below vocal line (bar 33)
  - Crotchets rising by step in violin I (bar 40)
  - Sustained, syncopated viola line, broadly a 3rd below vocal line (bar 54)
  - Cello doubles vocal line (bar 58)
  - Contrapuntal combination of introductory line with chorus (bar 63).

Tempo, metre and rhythm

- Fast quadruple time (136 crotchet beats a minute)
- Strict time throughout until the slight ritenuto at the close
- Insistent repeated crotchets plus quavers (see bars 3–4)
- Sustained notes appear in the cellos
- Syncopation (bars 2, 9–11, 20–21).

Melody

- The melody is modally ambiguous:
  - The F♯ over a C major chord (bar 1) implies lydian mode
  - C♯ (bar 10) seems to indicate dorian mode, but the C♮ (bar 13) hints at aeolian mode
- The opening statement of the verse consists of five bars, subdivided thus:
  - Single opening bar with triadic descent, highlighting names of the characters (Eleanor Rigby and Father McKenzie)
  - Middle three bars are marked by descending sequence and syncopation
  - The final single bar of each phrase highlights the situation or the message (e.g. 'lives in a dream', 'who is it for?' 'no-one comes near', 'no-one was saved'):

Bars 9–13

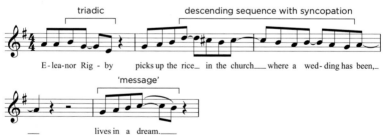

- The chorus melody avoids the 6th and 7th degrees of the scale, involving only 1st, 3rd, 4th and 5th notes
- Despair underlined by:
  - Upwards octave leap (bar 20)
  - Leap of a minor 10th (bar 24)
  - Close on the mediant (bar 25).

Harmony

- The song is built on two chords, E minor and C major, except for an A minor chord at bar 61

- Overall, the harmonic rhythm is slow, in marked contrast to the song's brisk pace.

Structure

- The song is in modified strophic form, with three verses, preceded by an introduction and followed by a chorus

- Each verse consists of three lines, with a sometimes loose rhyme scheme for lines 2 and 3, such as been-dream, door-for in verse 1.

Bars	Section	Details
1–8	Introduction	Two four-bar phrases, subdivided into two and a quarter bars vocal ('Ah, look at all the lonely people') and instrumental fill
9–18	Verse	Two five-bar statements, phrased 1 + 3 + 1 (repeated)
19–26	Chorus	Two four-bar phrases, subdivided into three bars vocal and one bar instrumental fill

Tonality

- E minor
- There are no modulations
- Notice the modal inflections (see Melody).

'Here, There and Everywhere'

According to McCartney, this love song was inspired by the Beach Boys' song 'God only knows'.

Sonority

The lead vocal is sung by McCartney, using automatic double-tracking, and supported by lead guitar, bass guitar, acoustic guitar, drums and vocals. In spite of the apparent simplicity of the sound, the multiple role played by McCartney (vocal, bass and acoustic guitars) and the three-part backing vocals would have required the blending of several takes.

Texture

- Melody-dominated homophony
- Guitar alternates between block chords and a broken-chord figuration
- Three-part supporting vocals ('Oo-') are heard in the verses
- A second vocal line is added in the last verse at bars 21–22
- A chromatic fill can be heard in bar 15.

Tempo, metre and rhythm

- Moderate 84 crotchets a minute
- Quadruple time, with a bar of $\frac{7}{8}$ in the introduction
- The introduction is performed rubato, before a steady pulse is established in bar 4
- The flexible speech-rhythms lead to
  - Notes carried over the starts of beats (see bar 5)
  - Scotch snaps (bar 13).

Melody

- Almost completely syllabic word-setting
- Broken triads in introduction, closing on dominant in preparation for the verse
- Unusual phrase structure in the verse of 1 + 2 + 2 + 3 bars
- The range is relatively wide (a 9th)
- The melody moves freely between monotone passages, conjunct movement and leaps.

Harmony

- Underlying harmonic rhythm is regular (2 + 2 + 1 + 1 + 1 + 1 bars)
- Frequent parallel movement, e.g. I–ii–iii–IV in the verse from bar 4
- A sudden shift to F♯ minor paves the way for a brief modulation to E minor
- In the bridge, the key of G minor is clearly defined by the iv –V⁷ progression in bars 14 and 16
- Plagal cadence at the close
- Other features include:
  - Appoggiatura at bar 5 (on 'each')
  - Dissonant E in bar 7 resolved by upward movement of the harmony
  - Brief false relation in bar 9 (C♮ in vocal and C♯ in harmony)
  - Harmonic sequence (bars 9–10).

Bars 4–11

Structure and tonality

Bars	Section	Key
1–3	Introduction	G – B♭ – V of G
4–11	Verse 1	G
4–12	Verse 2	G
13–16	Bridge 1	B♭ – G minor
17–24	Verse 3	G
13–16	Bridge 2	B♭ – G minor
17–25	Verse 4	G
25–30	Coda	G

'I Want to Tell You'

This number by George Harrison concerns 'the avalanche of thoughts that are so hard to write down or say or transmit'. The song's sense of frustration is evident in the markedly dissonant harmony.

Sonority

The number involved Harrison's double-tracked vocals and lead guitar, while McCartney provided bass guitar and piano.

A particular feature of the song is the three-part vocal harmonisation (e.g. 'My head is filled with things to say'), with Lennon and McCartney supporting Harrison. Besides the drum-kit, tambourine, maracas and handclaps are also heard.

Texture

The texture is melody-dominated homophony throughout.

Tempo, metre and rhythm

- Brisk number at 124 crotchets a minute
- Quadruple time
- Jazz quavers are present in the guitar riff which also features triplet crotchets

> The expression 'jazz quavers' means that in place of straight quavers, the notes are performed unevenly, i.e. crotchet-quaver.

- Triplet quavers appear in the closing bar of the bridge
- Verses are typified by insistent crotchets on piano
- Syncopations occur in the vocal parts.

Melody

The song is built on a limited amount of material:

- It fades in with a guitar riff in which a flattened 7th is prominent:

Bars 1–2

- Fragmentary nature of the melody underlines the desperation of the lyrics
- Dislocated phrases of varying lengths, some as short as a bar, but extending to three and a half bars at the end of each verse
- The lead vocal has a range of a major 7th (E to D♯)
- In the bridge, the range of the vocal line is even more limited, moving from persistent monotone B ('But if I seem to act unkind'), to F♯ at bar 31, before closing on A
- Notice the use of melisma in the coda.

Harmony

The harmony hints at the difficulty of transmitting thoughts in the following ways:

- A limited number of chords (A, B⁷, E⁷, A)
- Dissonant acciaccaturas – C♮ on C♯) at bar 5, and D♮ on D♯ at bar 8
- The jolting effect of the sudden shift to the B⁷
- The jarringly dissonant E minor 9th (F♮ over E), regarded as one of the most remarkable effects in the Beatles' repertory
- The chords of the bridge convey a similarly claustrophobic feel, moving from B minor to B diminished and then A.

Structure and tonality

There is scarcely any deviation from the key of A major.

Bars	Section	Key
1–4 (repeated)	Introduction	A major
5–15	Verse 1	A
16–26	Verse 2	A
27–35	Bridge 1	(B minor) – A
16–26	Verse 3	A
27–34	Bridge 2	(B minor) – A
16–25	Verse 3 repeated	A
36–45	Coda	A

'Tomorrow Never Knows'

The text of this number was assembled by Lennon and was based on *The Psychedelic Experience: A Manual Based on the Tibetan Book of the Dead* **by Timothy Leary, Richard Alpert, and Ralph Metzner.**

According to Harrison, it was to do with meditation which went beyond waking, sleeping and dreaming in the quest for pure consciousness, freed from the clutter of the physical world.

Sonority

The number has a unique sound quality resulting from complex studio engineering. Some typical devices include:

- Treatment of Lennon's vocal part; the opening stanzas were recorded with automatic double-tracking
- The verses after the instrumental were distorted by being run through a revolving Leslie speaker (found in Hammond organs) as Lennon wished to sound like chanting Tibetan monks

- Use of tape loops, of which the following are audible in the course of the song:
  - The 'seagull' effect which was actually a speeded-up tape of McCartney (first heard at c. 0:08)
  - An orchestral chord of B♭ major (0:19)
  - An electric guitar phrase, reversed and played at double speed (0:22)
  - Sitar-like sound, reversed and played at double speed (0:56).

Only one take was made, as the assembly of this material was inevitably aleatoric.

Aleatoric music is music in which chance plays a role, very often through the rhythmic freedom allowed the performers. Its use became widespread in the 1960s, notably in the work of the Polish composer Witold Lutosławski.

Texture

- Solo voice supported by continuous drone C with bass guitar riff from bar 3
- Drums heard throughout
- A web of tape loops produces an electronic polyphony with occasional homophony (the chords of B♭ and C).

Tempo, metre and rhythm

- Tempo of the vocal part is moderate
- Syncopation
- Triplet crotchets
- Triplet quavers in the guitar solo loop
- Dotted rhythms and scotch snap can also be heard in this solo.

Melody

- The melody is phrased 4 + 2 + 2 bars
- The opening bars outline the tonic broken chord with elemental effect
- The two last phrases move from 5th degree up to flattened 7th and then tonic
- Flattened 3rds can be heard in the tape loops (bar 23).

Harmony

Besides the drone, the only other harmonic element is the presence of two chords, B♭ moving to C.

Structure and tonality

The key is C, with prominent flattened 7th.

The song is strophic and its basic structure is as follows:

- Faded-in introduction
- Three verses of eight bars each
- Instrumental (16 bars)
- Four verses
- Coda, focused on repetitions of the final bars of the verse
- Outro (fade).

AREA OF STUDY 5:
Fusions

Estampes: No. 1: 'Pagodes' and No. 2: 'La Soirée dans Grenade' (Debussy)

Context

- *Estampes* ('*Prints*') was written in 1903
- It was the first of Debussy's piano works to be regarded as truly impressionistic – a term first applied to the work of such painters as Monet
- Notice in this respect:
  - Emphasis on colour and texture
  - Use of the piano's sustain pedal to blend sonorities
  - Music that was not designed to be programmatic so much as allusive
- There are three pieces in *Estampes*, the last of which (not prescribed here) is 'Jardins sous la pluie' ('Gardens in the rain'), based on a French folk song
- The prescribed works show influences of Indonesian gamelan music ('Pagodes') and Spanish music ('La soirée dans Grenade')
- Debussy first became acquainted with the Javanese gamelan at the Paris World Exhibition in 1889, and it clearly influenced the sonority and melodic content of 'Pagodes' (use of pentatonic scale).

Regarding programmatic music, Debussy once remarked that music should not be 'confined to reproducing, more or less exactly, Nature, but the mysterious correspondences which link Nature with Imagination'. In reality, this approach is more symbolist than impressionist, as the work of art becomes a symbol of a concept or idea, rather than a specific evocation of the real world.

Notation

- 'Pagodes' is notated throughout on the two staves typically used in piano music
- 'La Soirée dans Grenade' resorts to three staves at bars 96–109 and bars 130–end

- Conventional dynamic marks are employed
- Many other performance directions are in French, though Debussy uses some Italian (e.g. *rubato, tempo giusto*)
- Vague pedal directions are given in 'Pagodes' and are only specifically printed for the last seven bars of 'La soirée dans Grenade'. However, from the style of writing, it is clear that the sustaining pedal is essential throughout. '2 Ped' indicates sustain pedal and una corda ('soft pedal') together.

Sonority

- Both pieces use very nearly the full range of the piano:
  - In 'Pagodes' from lowest B to highest A♯
  - In 'La soirée dans Grenade' from lowest C♯ to top C♯
- Washes of sound are created in 'Pagodes' through use of sustaining pedal
- A more brittle staccato articulation is used on occasion in 'La Soirée dans Grenade'
- Una corda pedal contributes to the characteristic timbre of 'Pagodes'.

> Una corda is the left-foot pedal on the piano, which aids the creation of a softer, almost muffled sound.

Textures

'Pagodes'

The textures vary considerably in density and type, with dynamics ranging from delicate at the start to massive fortissimo at the climax:

- Layered homophony (bars 1–2)
- Melody-dominated homophony (bar 3) with double pedal (drone)
- Melody-dominated homophony with additional inner part (bar 7)
- Two-part counterpoint (bar 11)
- Brief imitation (bar 23)
- Left-hand chords with a high, bell-like right hand
- Rapid ornamental right-hand figuration, melody in middle range, long bass notes (bar 78).

'La Soirée dans Grenade'

The texture draws on various types of homophony, often layered; dynamics range from *ppp* to *ff*.

Notice particularly the following features:

- Monophonic – melody in left hand with inverted pedal in right hand (bar 7)
- Chords with single sustained bass note (bar 17)
- Homophonic; melody in octaves (bar 38)
- Three layers – melody transferred to middle part, chords above, habanera rhythm in bass (bar 51).

Tempo, metre and rhythm

'Pagodes'

- The tempo is 'modérément animé' (moderately quickly), with frequent use of ritardando
- The time signature is simple quadruple ($\frac{4}{4}$), with two bars of $\frac{2}{4}$ (bars 92 and 94)
- Notice the following features:
  - Syncopation (e.g. bar 1)
  - Tied notes over bar lines, undermining a strong sense of first-beat accent (e.g. bars 3–4)
  - Triplets (e.g. bar 11)
  - Quintuplets (e.g. bar 80)
  - Hetero-rhythms, or cross-rhythms, typically twos against threes (e.g. bar 23), eight demi-semiquavers against three quavers (e.g. bar 78)
  - Long gong-like sounds in bass.

'La Soirée dans Grenade'

A distinguishing feature in this piece is its habanera rhythm:

- Debussy indicates that the tempo is 'movement de Habanera', and that the piece should begin slowly in a nonchalantly graceful rhythm ('Commencer lentement dans un rhythme nonchalamment gracieux')
- It is in duple time ($\frac{2}{4}$), with sudden switches to triple time ($\frac{3}{4}$) at bars 109 and 115

- There are also indications that the performer should alternate between *rubato* and *tempo giusto* (strict time)
- Note also the following rhythmic features:
  - Triplets (e.g. bars 9 and 15)
  - Syncopation (e.g. bars 11, 33–36, 67)
  - Hetero-rhythm (twos against threes) (e.g. bar 34)
  - Scotch snaps (e.g. bars 35 and 36).

Melody

'Pagodes'

Much of the melody is built on:

- Two-bar phrases
- Pentatonic structures
- Its first melodic line consists of just four pitches: G#–C#–D#–F#; the fifth note of this pentatonic scale (B) is supplied in the accompanying harmonic structure:

Pagodes, bar 3 (melody and bass only)

This melody is rhythmically varied through the introduction of triplets at bar 11.

- A change of pentatonic pattern in the melody at bars 15–18 to G#–A#–C#–D#–F
- A whole-tone element occurs in the melody of the central section (bar 33): see the line E#–D#–C#–B
- A final pentatonic motif can be heard at bar 37, drawing on the original set of pitches.

'La Soirée dans Grenade'

This piece is built on a limited number of melodic motifs:

- The orientalist 'Andalusian'-Arabic melody at bar 7. Note particularly the lining up of semitone and augmented 2nd (bracketed in the example on the next page).

La Soirée dans Grenade, bars 7–16 (melody only)

- Other features of the melody above include:
  - Acciaccaturas
  - A limited range (an octave, with much of the melody in the upper half)
  - Avoidance of balanced phrasing
- Theme 2 at bar 17 featuring:
  - Balanced two-bar phrases
  - Repeated notes
- Theme 3 at bar 23, featuring whole-tone elements
- Extension of theme 2 with a loose descending sequence built on descending 3rds (bars 33–36)
- Theme 4 (bar 41) in major mode with lengthy descent:

La Soirée dans Grenade, bars 41–50 (melody)

Harmony

'Pagodes'

The harmony in this piece is strongly affected by the pentatonic content of the melody.

Significant aspects include:

- Its static quality
- Slow harmonic rhythm

- 'Changing background' approach, i.e. changing harmonisations of the same melody
- The added 6th (B–D♯–F♯–G♯) at the start

Other prominent landmarks include:

- Extended chords, e.g. B^{13} (bar 7)
- Diminished triad (bar 16^2)
- Colouristic, isolated major 2nd (bar 32)
- Pentatonic harmonisation at bar 37, with parallelism and open 5th chords.

'La Soirée dans Grenade'

The harmonic vocabulary is much more varied in this piece than in 'Pagodes'.

Typical devices include:

- Pedal points
- Parallel 7th chords (e.g. bar 17)
- Whole-tone harmonies (e.g. bar 23)
- False relations between adjacent chords (e.g. bar 33)
- Open 5ths chords (e.g. bar 38)
- Chords of 5ths and 4ths (bar 38, last quaver)
- Simultaneous false relation (e.g. bar 52)
- Parallel triads (bars 109–110).

Structure and tonality

'Pagodes'

- Ternary form with coda
- Static harmonies mean that it remains close to B major, though the central section (bars 33–53) moves into the region of F♯ major/D♯ minor.

'La Soirée dans Grenade'

- A succession of different themes, with some repetition
- The opening 'Arabic' theme returns at the end and closes in the tonic major
- The major mode theme (beginning bar 38) is repeated once (beginning bar 97)
- Most keys are related to the tonic of F♯ minor
- Keys are reinforced through the use of pedal points
- Tonality is weakened, however, by the use of whole-tone harmony
- The two interruptions in triple time also contrast dramatically, by being in the keys of C mixolydian (bar 109) and A mixolydian (bar 115).

'Allá va candela' and 'Se quema la chumbambá' from *Caña Quema*: (La Familia Valera Miranda)

Context

- The two prescribed excerpts are examples of Cuban music from the Oriente region in the east of the country, which has Santiago de Cuba as its main city
- The fusion of styles here involves a blending of an essentially European (Spanish) element with Latin American features, some of which also had links with African music
- The Spanish element is evident in the use of guitars, cuatro and double bass, and the use of a functional harmonic language
- The Afro-Cuban influence is evident in the use of maracas, bongos and claves
- The two songs date back to the early part of the 20th century and were the work of earlier generations of La Familia Valera Miranda, the performers of the excerpts.

La Familia Valera Miranda (the Valera Miranda family) in the 19th century worked on the land, producing sugar cane and trees for timber; several members of the family were involved in the struggle against Spanish colonialists, culminating in the establishing of the independent Republic of Cuba in 1902.

- Cuban music is often intended for dancing and usually originated in improvisation
- Subject matter could be political, or humorous retellings of incidents in the life of the family:
  - 'Se quema la chumbambá' ('Our land is burning') is concerned with the family matriarch's dismissive reaction to news that a fire had broken out on the Valera's farm
  - 'Allá va candela' ('There goes Mr Fire') mocks one of the members of the band who had fallen madly in love
- The band consists of vocalists, guitar, cuatro, double bass and percussion instruments (bongos, maracas, claves).

Notation

- Both songs are initially notated in full score in the Anthology
- Once basic patterns are established in the accompanying section, large parts of each song are given in reduced form – i.e. only the vocal part is given in 'Se quema la chumbambá' and vocal part with cuatro in 'Allá va candela'
- Significant changes in the other instruments are notated when they arise, and the conclusions of both songs are given in full score
- The cuatro solos in both songs are notated in full
- Tempo indications are in beats per minute
- There are a limited number of traditional dynamic marks and accent signs.

Dance types

Cuban music included such types of dance as habanera (see Debussy's 'La Soirée dans Grenade'), canción, son and bolero. 'Se quema la chumbambá' is a son (regarded as a forerunner of the salsa), while 'Allá va candela' opens as a bolero before morphing into a son.

Son characteristics:

- Use of call and response
- Duple metre
- 3-2 son clave pattern forming a two-bar pattern with three notes in the first and two in the second:

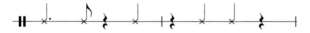

- A limited harmonic scheme, typically of tonic and dominant chords
- Vocal part based on Spanish metrical patterns
- Strophic structure, perhaps with instrumental part-way through.

Bolero characteristics:

- Associated with romantic subjects
- Moderate duple time (as distinct from the European bolero in triple time)
- The bolero tends to be more lyrical than the son.

Sonority

- Performing forces in both numbers are:
  - Solo male voice (Pregón) and male-voice chorus (Coro)
  - Cuatro (a guitar-like instrument with four 'courses' (sets) of two strings)
  - Guitar

- Plucked double bass
- Maracas, claves and bongo.

Texture

- Melody-dominated homophony predominates in both songs
- The coro in 'Se quema' is homophonic (homorhythmic), with the two parts singing in 3rds, 6ths, diminished 5ths and perfect 4ths
- In 'Allá va candela', the coro is confined to interjections of two notes in octaves
- Monophony (cuatro) can be heard at the opening of both songs
- The cuatro solos in both songs involve some multi-stopping.

Tempo, metre and rhythm

'Se quema la chumbambá'

- Brisk duple time
- 3-2 son claves (see example above in 'son characteristics')
- Constant quavers on bongo
- Syncopation (e.g. cuatro solo, bar 83)
- A three-crotchet rhythm every fourth bar of vocals
- Triplets in passing in cuatro solo.

'Allá va candela'

- Moderate duple time, typical of bolero-son at start
- An accelerando at bar 39 leads into the brisker son
- Flowing quavers on cuatro at start
- Anacrusis in vocal part
- Dotted rhythms
- Syncopations (cuatro, bar 5).

Melody

Both numbers are characterised by balanced phrasing.

'Se quema la chumbambá'

- Vocal lines draw on first six notes of G minor scale
- The lead vocal's line begins on the dominant
- Cuatro introduction uses broken chord patterns
- Chromatic elements and bigger leaps appear in cuatro solo.

'Allá va candela'

- Vocal lines draw on all notes within the scale of E major
- Solo vocal line spans a 12th (B–F♯)
- Falling 5ths at ends of phrases
- Rapidly repeated notes represent a feverishly beating heart
- Cuatro's solo is marked by chromaticism (bars 75–76) and ornamentation (acciaccaturas and slides).

Harmony

A limited range of chords is used in both songs.

'Se quema la chumbambá'

- Tonic and dominant 7th chords
- Additional E♭ on cuatro creates a brief dominant 9th and outlines of diminished 7th chords
- C major is touched on in the cuatro solo at bars 89–90.

'Allá va candela'

- Tonic (with occasional added 6th) in cuatro and dominant 7th (plus 9th)
- Harmony expanded with reference to subdominant (e.g. bar 29)
- Cuatro ranges more widely with parallel 4ths (bar 75) and V^{11} (bar 79)

Structure and tonality

'Se quema la chumbambá'

- G minor without modulation
- Alternating verse and refrain, broken at one point by an extended cuatro solo.

'Allá va candela'

- E major without modulation
- The structure is less regular than that of 'Se quema', as follows:
  - Introduction and bolero material ('Tengo la boca' and 'Corazón'), which is not subsequently repeated
  - 'Desde los pies' (bars 32–38)
  - Allá va candela chorus – solo vocal and coro (repeated)
  - Extended cuatro solo
  - Truncated reference to chorus (bars 124–138) followed by repeat of 'Desde los pies'
  - Repeat of 'Allá va candela' chorus (solo vocal and coro) with solo vocal improvisation.

Breathing Under Water: 'Burn', 'Breathing Under Water' and 'Easy' (Anoushka Shankar)

Context

- Anoushka Shankar, born in 1981, is the daughter of the celebrated Indian musician Ravi Shankar

- Anoushka Shankar learned sitar with her father and has also gained recognition as a composer

- Her earliest recordings – *Anoushka* (1998) and *Anourag* (2000) – draw on the ragas of Northern Indian classical music

- Later albums – *Rise* (2005) and *Breathing Under Water* (2007) – include her own compositions and are distinguished by the presence of jazz and pop elements

- *Breathing Under Water* was written in collaboration with:

  - The table drummer, Utkarsha Kale

  - Bollywood film composer, Salim Merchant

  - Gaurav Raina

  - Composer and singer, Norah Jones, the half-sister of Anoushka

- The album is a fascinating fusion of classical sitar and other Indian instruments, traditional Indian vocal styles, electronic drums, synthesised sounds, atmospheric Bollywood-style sonorities, and 'Western' pop elements evident in the use of electric guitar and piano as well as some aspects of the harmonic language.

Notation

- The scores were made on the basis of the recorded sound, some elements of which would have been improvised

- In 'Burn' and 'Breathing Under Water', the basic layout consists of two staves for the strings in short score, with additional stave for sitar

- In 'Burn', additional staves are added for sarangi, percussion, synthesised bass and vocals (with up to three voices notated at a time)

- In 'Burn', parts for brass, harp, flute and solo cello are included on the strings staves as required, and in 'Breathing Under Water' a note on the score (bar 18) indicates the addition of woodwind, brass and double bass

- In all three numbers, guitar chords are given above the system

- Tempi are given by metronome indications at the start of each number;

otherwise there are no further speed indications

- A limited number of traditional (Italian) dynamic marks are given
- Repeated figures are indicated by ⅌
- In 'Easy' the strings are replaced by piano (single stave) and guitar. 'Pad' effects and electronic drums are given on separate staves.

'Burn'

The lyrics concern the mystery of love as reflected in the moon, sun and stars and expressed in the dance.

Sonority

- The basic soundworld consists of strings, sitar and vocals
- A sarangi is introduced in bars 46–53
- Orchestral additions include brass (bar 94), harp (bar 102), flute (bar 104) and cello (bar 107)
- Percussion instruments include:
  - Bass drum (bar 14)
  - Manjira (hand cymbals) (bar 22)
  - Drum kit (bar 22)
  - Ride cymbal (bar 29)
- Ethereal synth pad is used at bar 30.

A **sitar** is a long-necked string instrument with a gourd resonator. Its six or seven main strings are plucked with a metal plectrum, and its characteristic timbre is produced by the additional sympathetic strings which resonate in sympathy with the main strings.

A **sarangi** is a bowed string instrument with three main strings and up to 36 sympathetic strings.

Texture

- The basic texture (as heard at the opening) is melody-dominated homophony with the sitar's melody accompanied by chords in the strings accompaniment
- These chords vary in density, and as the piece develops, additional melodic content appears in the strings, e.g. bars 14–21
- Octaves appear in the string melody at bar 14

- A lively synth bass octaves figure is added at bar 22

- At bar 22, a percussion ostinato is introduced

- The vocal part (bar 30) is initially a single line, but later (e.g. bar 54) is doubled a 3rd below

- A third voice part is added at the climax (e.g. bar 99)

- Texture is thinned down to two parts at bar 86

- Densest textures occur at the climax, starting at bar 98.

Dynamics

- The loudest point (*ff*) occurs at bar 98

- Elsewhere the dynamic is relatively soft, although there are crescendos into the start of new sections (e.g. bar 37).

Tempo, metre and rhythm

- **Tempo** is 80 crotchets a minute without variation of pulse

- The quadruple ($\frac{4}{4}$) **metre** remains constant throughout, but the opening section (bars 1–21) has the slow, freely improvised qualities of the *alap* which opens the traditional *rāg* with an exploration of the scale to be used presented in a rhythmically-free style. It is followed at bar 22 with a stricter approach to rhythm, involving percussion, which perhaps recalls the *jhala* section of the *rāg*

- Initially the strings have relatively long, sustained chords while the sitar is characterised by the following **rhythmic** features:

  - Dotted rhythm (bar 3–5)

  - Triplets, both crotchets (bar 6) and quavers (bars 10–11)

  - Syncopation (bar 23)

  - Quintuplet (bar 57)

- The vocal line has a tighter, more regular rhythmic pattern, although it still features triplets, syncopations, etc

- The percussion ostinato (from bar 22), in its limited rhythmic repetitions, is more characteristic of Western music.

Melody

The sitar covers a wide range in this number, extending from G♯ in bass to E two octaves above middle C in treble.

- The sitar's melody is in the (Western) key of C♯ minor (with some B♯s) rather than a scale associated with one of the *rāgs*

- It opens with a clearly defined descending line (bar 5):

Bars 3–5

- There is much typical ornamentation:
  - Microtonal slides
  - 'Crushed' notes
  - Mordents of varying durations.

Vocals

- The range is initially limited to just a 6th (C#–A). Notice the loose sequence:

Bars 30–39

- Later a lower part touches on B# and an additional line extends up to C#.

Strings

- Initially the uppermost part has a range of just a 5th, from C♯ to G♯, and eventually extending to A at bar 18
- The line starting at bar 18 seems to anticipate the vocal line at bars 30–31:

Bars 18–21

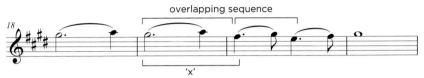

Sarangi at bar 46 also seems to relate to the strings at bar 18 and vocals at bar 30:

Bar 46

Harmony

There is an avoidance of cadential harmony, but notice the near-perfect cadence at bars 73–74 (G♯sus4)–C♯sus4)/E♯).

Other features include:

- Slow harmonic rhythm
- Often quietly dissonant language
- Root position chords (bar 87)
- Sus chords, as in the example given above
- Slash chords, some resulting in inversions (e.g. second inversion in bar 9)
- Added note chords (e.g. bar 6)
- Relatively frequent A^7 – C♯ progression
- C♯ is present throughout, but at bar 22 takes the form of a tonic pedal.

Tonality

- 'Burn' is in C♯ minor with aeolian elements
- But closes on an open 5ths D chord
- The constant C♯s elsewhere could be likened to the tanpura-like drone of traditional classical Indian music.

Structure

'Burn' loosely follows a verse and chorus form with introduction, instrumentals and coda:

Bars 1–29	Introduction	*'Alap'* leading to rhythmically stricter *'jhala'* (bar 22)
Bars 30–37	Verse 1 ('Dancing...')	Two four-bar phrases
Bars 38–45	Chorus 1 ('Dance with me')	Three-fold repetition of one-bar pattern with linking phrase ('Search with me...')
Bars 46–53	Bridge	Sarangi solo
Bars 54–65	Verse 2 ('Falling...')	Vocals now in 3rds
Bars 66–77	Bridge	Extended and varied through interpolation of instrumental motif from introduction (bar 14) at bar 66, and reintroduction of strings melody from bar 18 at bar 70 combining with 'Your eyes close...'
Bars 78–97	Verse 3 ('Dancing...') and bridge modified	Extended by way of sitar and strings instrumental (bar 86); and material from bridge ('Your eyes close...') at bar 94
Bars 98–104	Chorus	Climax
Bars 105–110	Coda	New timbres (flute and cello) and a close out of key on open 5ths D

'Breathing Under Water'

Vocals

This number is largely instrumental with intermittent vocalisation (i.e. wordless singing).

Sonorities

The number requires:

- Sitar solo
- String accompaniment, sometimes reinforced with woodwinds, horns and additional double bass
- Female vocals
- Flute
- Cello
- Tabla (at bar 27)

Texture

- Monophony (female voice) at bars 35–36
- Two-part (voice and sitar) at bars 36–37
- At bar 54, a more distinct melodic strand can be heard in upper strings, over which the sitar and vocals can be heard in free counterpoint.

Dynamics

Dynamic levels are low throughout:

- *mp/p* on sitar and strings at the start
- *pp* for female voice.

Tempo, metre and rhythm

- **Tempo** is 120 crotchets a minute
  - In spite of the 'surface' activity in the sitar and vocal parts, the number creates a slow, spacious impression with long held string chords
- The **metre** is simple quadruple ($\frac{4}{4}$) throughout except for a single bar of $\frac{2}{4}$ at bar 37
- **Rhythm** at the background level is characterised by slow-moving, long-sustained chords
- The sitar part is free and highly varied:
  - Scotch snaps (bar 2)
  - Triplets (bar 6)

- Quintuplets (bar 12)
- Syncopation (bars 5–6).

Melody

- The sitar melody is notated within the scales of ('Western') D♭ major and C♯ aeolian
- Apart from microtonal slides, chromatic notes occur, e.g. C♭ (bars 7–8) and F♭ (bar 17)
- The sitar melody lies in a generally higher tessitura than 'Burn', with bass clef only being applied in bars 61–67
- Overall sitar range is two octaves and a third: D♭ below middle C to F an octave and a half above middle C
- Though the overall impression is one of improvisatory freedom, a number of melodic phrases are repeated almost exactly, e.g. compare:
  - Bars 1–4 with bars 36–40
  - Bars 9–14 with bars 45–49
  - Bars 19–20 with bars 23–24
- There are numerous ornamentations:
  - Mordents
  - Crushed notes (acciaccaturas)
  - Glissandi, introducing microtonal slides.

Many of the rhythmic and melodic features mentioned above appear in the following example. You may find it helpful to mark them in.

Bars 1–8

Vocals

- The melody is notated in C♯ minor, although with major mode inflections (e.g. bar 37, preparing for a move back to D♭ major)
- The first vocal melody is characterised by a conjunct descending line spanning a 6th (bars 35–37), then at bars 42–45, only a 4th
- A contrasting, still conjunct, line is heard in D♭ major at bar 55
- Microtonal slides appear at bar 64
- Appoggiatura (G♭) in final bar.

Strings

In bars 54–67, the strings have a clearer melodic line (in minims throughout), moving by step for the most part.

Harmony

- Slow harmonic rhythm
- Apart from the final plagal cadence, there is an absence of cadential harmony
- Root position chords, e.g. bars 2–3
- Sus4 chord (bar 4)
- Added note chords, e.g. added 9th at bar 7
- Some parallelism, e.g. bars 27–28.

Tonality

- The number is in D♭, but starts obliquely in B♭ minor
- D♭ tonality is veiled at bar 16 by the D♭$^{(sus4)}$ chord and the F♭s in the sitar, giving a minor mode inflection at bar 17
- From bars 18 to 37, the signature indicates the tonic minor, though tonality here is vague and in fact this section ends on an A minor chord
- Bars 38 to 77 return to the region of D♭.

Structure

The number is an exploration of a number of distinctive ideas, partly differentiated by broad contrasts of tonality. In broad terms there are four sections and a short coda.

Bars 1–18	D♭	There is a distinct feeling of balanced four-bar phrases in this first main section: A A¹ B B¹ (extended to link with the next section)
Bars 18–35	C♯	Four-bar phrasing continues in the accompanying parts, but though the sitar also has four-bar phrases, they are out of synch with the accompaniment, being one bar later. A new motif enters at bar 27 in sitar, and a further new line enters in voice at bar 35, overlapping with a return of the opening material.
Bars 35–53	D♭	A variation of the opening section, co-ordinated with voice
Bars 53–70	D♭	Further elaboration of the sitar's earlier material, combined with vocals and a most effective slow-moving melody in strings. In the Anthology recording, the bass movement from G down to F occurs in bar 60, not in bar 59 as shown in the Anthology, and the chord in bar 60 would seem to be best described as a first inversion D♭ major chord, rather than Fm.
Bars 71–77	D♭	Coda: notice the chromatic line in the cello solo at bar 75 and the plagal cadence (G♭m⁶–D♭)

'Easy'

Music and lyrics are by Norah Jones.

Lyrics: a slightly world-weary number telling us that as we get older, love is not everything: 'it's only love and feeling is easy'.

Sonorities

This most 'Western' sounding of the three numbers to be studied is scored for:

- Piano
- Electric guitar
- Warm pad

- Sitar
- Vocals (up to three parts, e.g. bar 23)
- Synth bass
- Percussion, including
  - Electronic drums
  - Shaker
  - Manjira (hand cymbals).

Texture

- Melody-dominated homophony, first with sitar as the main melody instrument
- Subsequently vocals take the melody line with fills on sitar
- Texture is varied by addition and subtraction of colouristic elements and percussion.

Dynamics

- Levels are relatively low with few indications:
  - $\boldsymbol{p}$ at start
  - *cresc.* at bar 21
  - $\boldsymbol{mp}$ at bar 25
- Accent marks are used in bar 43.

Tempo, metre and rhythm

- **Tempo** is 84 crotchets a minute, without variation
- **Metre** is simple quadruple ($\frac{4}{4}$) throughout except for bar 31 which is in $\frac{3}{4}$
- **Rhythm:**
  - Sitar rhythms are similar to those of the other numbers, but notice the septuplet in bar 20
  - The accompaniment is marked by syncopation and a rhythmic ostinato:

Bar 2

  - Vocals are also marked by syncopation, as well as use of:
    - Scotch snap
    - 1½ beat anacrusis

Bars 8–11

Melody

Sitar

- Notated throughout in treble, with a range of just over two octaves, from E♭ below middle C to F an octave and a 4th above middle C
- Characteristic devices used here are very similar to those already noted above (i.e. ornamentation and glissandi)
- It is notated throughout in G♭ without chromaticism.

Vocals

- The range of the lead vocal is relatively narrow, spanning a 6th (D♭ to B♭) in the first verse, though in the second verse a melisma extends down to a lower A♭ (bar 13), and in the middle 8 rises to a C♭ (bar 46)
- Backing vocals span a 9th, from F below middle C to G♭ above (see bars 29–32)
- Vocal lines are frequently conjunct, with leaps for the most part restricted to 3rds and 4ths; there is an octave at bar 44
- The underlay is a mixture of syllabic, slurred pairs of notes and melismas.

Harmony

- Based throughout on three sus chords:
    - D♭(sus4)
    - G♭(sus2)/B♭
    - C♭(sus2)
- The result, once the number is under way, is a stepwise rising bass (B♭–C♭–D♭)
- Variations in chord order occur in bars 29–33 and in the middle 8 (bars 42–49)
- The limited chord choice and its treatment results in a more obvious 'Western' pop sound.

Tonality

The tonality has an ambiguous floating quality, and though could be regarded as D♭ mixolydian, it is as likely that it is as much in G♭ with a strong pull to the dominant (D♭).

Structure

Bars 1-8	Instrumental introduction	
Bars 8^3-20	Verse 1 ('It's only love...')	Four vocal phrases (to bar 17), overlapping with sitar fill (from bar 18^2)
Bars 20-33^4	Verse 2 ('When I was young...')	Verse followed by linking passage featuring backing vocals ('I know')
Bars 33^4-42^1	Instrumental	Solo sitar
Bars 42^2-49^2	Middle 8	Wider vocal range and modified chord progression
Bars 49^3-57^2	Verse 3 ('It's only love...')	
Bars 57^3-63	Coda	Closes on D♭$^{(sus4)}$

FURTHER LISTENING

George Harrison, 'Within You Without You' (*Sgt. Pepper's Lonely Hearts Club Band*).

AREA OF STUDY 6:
New directions

Three Dances for Two Prepared Pianos: No. 1 (John Cage)

Context

- John Cage (1912–1992) was an American avant-garde composer
- He was a pupil of Henry Cowell (1897–1965), who experimented with extreme chromaticism, rhythmic complexity, graphic notation and extended piano techniques
- Some of Cage's most notable works stemmed from his work as an accompanist for the dancer and choreographer, Merce Cunningham
- An interest in providing percussion music for dance led Cage to develop the 'prepared piano' in an attempt to economise on both space and expense
- A prepared piano involved alteration of the piano's timbres through insertion of various items between the strings
- His most famous prepared piano work is *Sonatas and Interludes* (1948)
- The prescribed work – for two amplified prepared pianos – was completed in 1945 and was eventually used for dance purposes by Cunningham in *Dromenon* (1947)
- Cage's works reflect interests in:
  - Eastern philosophy and religion (*Sonatas and Interludes*)
  - The role of silence (*4'33"*)
  - Aleatoric music, or 'chance music' (*Music of Changes*).

Notation

- Full score with traditional staff notation
- Notice, however, that accidentals apply only to the note they precede and not to the whole bar
- Boxed numerals above the score act as reference points, indicating the start of a new phrase in the underlying structure
- Tempo is indicated by beats per minute
- Conventional dynamic indications are used

- In the Anthology, pedals are indicated with the directions 'una corda' ('quiet pedal'), 'tre corde' (end quiet pedal) and the standard 'Ped' sign to refer to the sustaining pedal.
- The score is preceded by instructions for preparing the instrument for performance.

Sonority

- Sonority and timbre depend on the preparations that Cage prescribed
- Preparation involves the insertion of so-called 'mutes' between the strings of the piano keys used
- Different materials are employed, e.g. metal bolts and screws, weather strip, rubber, plastic, coins
- Only the prepared notes appear in the course of the composition, and not all keys of the pianos have to be prepared
- A range of timbres results, from dead to gong-like
- Pitch, however, is distorted considerably, meaning that the score cannot be taken as a reliable guide to the resulting sound
- Though preparation instructions are detailed, it would be impossible to create the exact same effect from one performance to another.

Dynamics

- The dynamic level is mainly soft
- For extended sections there is little dynamic change (e.g. the opening part)
- There is an effective contrast between **ppp** just before phrase 36 and **ff** at phrase 38
- Accents are frequently employed (e.g. right hand of piano 1, phrases 38–40).

Texture

- The texture is mainly contrapuntal, with the two piano parts frequently working independently
- A two-part texture is used for each piano
- Other features to note include:
  - Monophony (phrase 5, from bar 14)
  - A sort of melody-dominated homophony (from phrase 38)
  - Homorhythm (from phrase 7).

Tempo, metre and rhythm

- Tempo is a fast duple time ($\frac{2}{2}$) throughout, at 88 minims per minute (not 88 crotchets per minute, as is written in the Anthology score)
- Note values are largely quavers and crotchets

- Duple metre is disrupted through cross-rhythms, mainly groupings of three quavers at a time (see piano 1 opening)
- Piano 2 works against piano 1's opening rhythm with a steady crotchet pattern in the left hand and off-beat quavers in the right hand
- Notice, however, that the left hand figure in piano 2 consists of a seven crotchet ostinato, also working against the written duple time.

Structure

- Like many works of this period, Cage's structure for this piece is based on a fractal mathematical approach, also known as micro-macrocosmic design
- Here the proportions used on a small scale also operate on the movement's overall structure:
  - Dance No. 1 consists of nine 30-bar parts
  - Each part is sub-divided into nine phrases, signalled by the boxed numerals in the score
  - The phrases in all parts have the following bar-lengths:
    2 5 2 – 2 6 2 – 2 7 2
  - It is highly unlikely that the listener is aware of these proportions in performance, but notice how the length of the central subdivision progressively increases by a bar a time (i.e. from 5 to 6 to 7)
- Thus, traditional large-scale dance forms are avoided, but there are some repetitions, e.g. the final 30-bar section is a repeat of the one preceding
- There are a number of other smaller-scale repetitions, including the reappearance of a number of motifs from the first two parts in the final parts, e.g. the three-quaver motif from phrase 5 returns at phrases 64 and 73.

Tonality

There can be no sense of tonality underpinning the movement's structure, given the nature of a prepared piano. In other words, there are no exact pitches creating a hierarchy of sounds revolving around a tonic.

Melody and harmony

For the same reason (indeterminate, unfixed pitch), it is impossible to speak of melodic line or harmonic content. In other words, rhythm and sonority prevail throughout.

FURTHER LISTENING

Try comparing Cage's approach to rhythm with Messiaen's use of iso-rhythms in e.g. *Quatuor pour le fin du temps*.

Petals [for Cello Solo and Optional Electronics] (Kaija Saariaho)

Context

- Kaija Saariaho is a leading Finnish composer, born in Helsinki in 1952
- She has produced a significant body of work in which electronics play an important role, e.g. the recent theatre piece *Only the Sound Remains* (2015)
- In *Petals*, the cello is combined with ongoing live electronics, as opposed to pre-recorded electronic sounds
- *Petals* was written for Anssi Karttunen, who first performed the work at a festival of contemporary music in Bremen in 1988
- The title of the work refers to the petal of the waterlily, and is an off-shoot of *Nymph*éa [*Waterlily*], dating from 1987, scored for string quartet and electronics
- According to the composer, *Petals* is concerned with the opposition of 'fragile colouristic passages' to 'more energetic events with clear rhythmic and melodic character', which in turn are subjected to a number of transformations.

Notation

- The basis of the score is conventional staff notation
- There are, however, no bars or bar numbers. Instead, each of the 30 lines in the piece is numbered, and we will refer to these lines as 'staves'
- Indications for use of reverb and harmoniser (see below) are placed under each stave
- At some points, the notation is indeterminate, i.e. aleatoric with regard to melodic and rhythmic elements
- Notation is expanded by the addition of various symbols indicating specific effects not covered by traditional notation, as follows:
  - Horizontal arrow – a gradual change from one sound or way of playing to another
  - Diminuendo hairpin closing with a small zero – reduction in volume to absolute silence
  - Crescendo hairpin starting with small zero – increase in volume, commencing from silence
  - Arrow-head pointing upwards – highest note possible
  - Filled in black crescendo sign – add bow pressure to produce a scratching sound, i.e. pitch is replaced by noise (and vice versa for diminuendo sign)

- See the introductory comments in the Anthology score for other symbols, notably those for quarter-tones and various types of glissando.

Sonority

- The work blends traditional cello timbres with extended techniques and various degrees of electronic distortion

Acoustic

- Traditional cello playing (bowed, pitched sound) can be heard in the music of staves 10–13
- Articulation includes slurs (e.g. stave 5) and staccato (e.g. stave 4)
- Extended techniques include:
  - Lengthy trills and tremolos for colouristic effect
  - Harmonics (usually artificial), often combined with ordinary notes (see stave 14) and more strikingly with another harmonic (stave 15)
  - Glissandos (with varying degrees of vibrato and/or with harmonics)
  - Micro-intervals
  - Scratchy tone (noise) produced by use of more bow pressure than usual.

Electronic

- Live electronics most importantly involve:
  - Digital reverb with variable reverb
  - Harmoniser
- Reverb time is set at 2.5 seconds, increasing to 15 seconds in stave 21 and finally 30 seconds at the close
- The introductory remarks in the Anthology state that the reverb should result in a 'clear and bright sound' and that if there is any doubt as to how much to apply, 'too little rather than too much' is preferable
- In any event, the degree of reverb varies between 20% and 50%
- The harmoniser shifts pitches by a quarter-tone and then combines this transposed sound with the original, typically during scratchy bowing sections to maximise colouristic distortion effects. (See introductory remarks for details on preferred models of harmoniser.)

Dynamics

The range is extreme: from sounds pulled out of silence, through *pppp* to *ffff*. Saariaho requires a 'clear and rich, close sound', stipulating that microphones should be placed as close as possible to the instrument and that the general level be set rather loud, but 'not painfully so'.

Texture

- In the more conventionally played passages, the cello line could be described as monophonic (e.g. stave 10)
- Double stopping occurs in stave 11 and is used to create harmonics in staves 14–16
- Effective use is made of two-part writing in stave 17, where the lowest string on the instrument (open C) is left ringing while material is played on higher strings
- Colouristic block-sounds result in the scratchy bowing passages with harmoniser, but these are far removed from the homophony of traditional textures. In fact, it is probably more useful to approach the topic of texture in terms of relative densities of sound.

Tempo, metre and rhythm

- **Tempo** moves between lento sections and faster moving passages
- *Lento* passages, as at the start, should move so slowly that staves in these sections should always last at least 20 seconds. The final section of the work is extremely slow, with the last stave taking at least 55 seconds to perform
- There is no **metre** discernable in terms of time signatures and bars
- Written note-lengths in the *lento* sections employ semibreves but are to be regarded as pulseless sounds of indeterminate length
- The passage beginning at stave 10 seems to be more precisely notated regarding **rhythms**, but pulse cannot be detected because of the irregularity of groupings, ornaments, ties, glissando and fermata (pauses).

Melody

- Melodic content is typically found in the faster moving sections (lento passages tend to be colouristic rather than melodic)
- In the energico section beginning at stave 4, a scurrying line can be heard, made up of quarter tones (microtones) and glissandos
- The second such section, at stave 10, is more conventionally melodic with clearly defined intervallic content, often of an angular nature (notice the intervals of a major 7th (stave 10) and augmented 4th (stave 12)
- Some other characteristics of this section include:
  - Repeated note figuration (stave 11)
  - Short descending figures (beginning on stave 11). The starting note of each descent rises, with the high-point occuring in stave 13
  - Ornamentation

- The poco impetuoso at stave 17 is characterised by agitated figures, initially semitonal
- From stave 23, striking use of glissandos rising alternately to C♯ and F♯ are supported by 'pedal' low (open string) Cs
- The section culminates with a glissando to the highest pitch available (stave 27).

Harmony

- There is no sense of harmonic progression, though there are very brief moments when distinguishable pitches are heard, e.g. stave 15
- It could be said that one traditional harmonic device is the lengthy pedal C at staves 15–28
- Notice the prominent high F♯s which appear at stave 23, seemingly forming a tritonal dominant with the pedal C.

> Tritonal dominants can be found in Herrmann's music for the film *Psycho*. Briefly they arise from the replacing of the traditional dominant with one an augmented 4th or diminished 5th above the tonic.

Tonality

- Tonality (in terms of a hierarchy of pitches) is scarcely relevant in *Petals*, partly because of the absence of functional harmonic progressions
- However, the persistent use of the pedal C from stave 15 could be regarded as a tonal anchor, even though the work is primarily colouristic.

Structure

- *Petals* is one continuous movement
- There are elements of short-term repetition of motifs. For example, the treatment of the glissando figures from stave 23
- The work depends on the alternation of what the composer describes as 'fragile colouristic passages' with 'more energetic events with clear rhythmic and melodic character':

Tempo	Staves
Lento	1–3
'energico'	4–7
Lento	8–9
'espressivo'	10–13
Lento	13–16
'poco impetuoso'	17–27
'dolcissimo' (This marking appears as 'Lento' in the original Hansen edition)	27–30

FURTHER LISTENING

It would be useful to investigate works by other Finnish composers:

- Sibelius, Symphonies Nos 4 and 5, and the tone poem *Tapiola*
- Rautavaara, *Cantus Arcticus* (scored for orchestra with pre-recorded birdsong)

For a fine example of another contemporary composer's approach to cello technique, listen to Lutosławski's Cello Concerto.

The Rite of Spring: Introduction, 'The Augurs of Spring' and 'Ritual of Abduction' (Stravinsky)

Context

- Igor Stravinsky (1882–1971), one of the leading Russian composers of the 20th century, was born in St Petersburg
- He studied with Nikolai Rimsky-Korsakov (1844–1908), the leading Russian nationalist composer of the time
- While training with Rimsky-Korsakov, Stravinsky completed a number of orchestral works, notably:
  - Symphony in E♭ (1907)
  - *Scherzo fantastique* (1908)
  - *Feu d'artifice* (1908)
- He attracted the attention of the celebrated impresario, Sergei Diaghilev, who commissioned a series of ballet scores:
  - *The Firebird* (1910)
  - *Petrouchka* (1911)
  - *The Rite of Spring* (1913)
- Stravinsky's early works are fine examples of the Russian nationalistic style, drawing heavily on folk song and revealing influences from such composers as Borodin, Mussorgsky and Rimsky-Korsakov
- In very general terms, the Russian national style differs from that of German composers of the time in a tendency to use:
  - Varied repetition rather than motivic development
  - Structures composed of contrasting blocks of sound
  - Changing backgrounds (harmonic and orchestral)
  - Vivid colouristic effects in general.

The Rite of Spring (also called *Le sacre du printemps* in French)

- *The Rite* originated in the composer's dream or 'fleeting vision' of a 'young maiden dancing to the point of exhaustion before a group of men of fabulous age'

- The underlying concept was developed in collaboration with the artist and designer, Nikolai Roerich (1874–1947), a leading specialist on Russian pagan antiquity
- The ballet eventually consisted of a series of 'pictures from pagan Russia' in two parts: 'The Adoration of the Earth' and 'The Great Sacrifice'
- The prescribed extracts, from 'The Adoration of the Earth', transport us to 'the foot of a sacred hill, amid green fields where Slavonic tribes have gathered for their vernal games…' (Roerich)
- The orchestral Introduction is a 'swarm of spring pipes' (dudki – 'dudki' being both Polish and Russian for wind pipes)
- It is followed by 'Augurs of Spring' ('Les augures printaniers') and 'Ritual of Abduction' ('Jeu du rapt')
- *The Rite of Spring* was first performed on 29 May 1913 at the Théâtre des Champs-Elysées in Paris, and provoked brawls among the audience.

Notation and musical terminology

- *The Rite* is notated as a full score with traditional (mainly Italian) terminology and dynamic markings
- Many transposing instruments are employed, i.e.:
  - Piccolo (sounding an octave higher than written)
  - Alto flute in G (sounding a perfect 4th lower than written)
  - Cor anglais and horn in F (sounding a perfect 5th lower than written)
  - Clarinet in B♭ (sounding a tone lower than written)
  - Clarinet in A (sounding a minor 3rd lower than written)
  - Piccolo clarinet in D (sounding a tone higher than written)
  - Piccolo clarinet in E♭ (sounding a minor 3rd higher than written)
  - Bass clarinet in B♭ (sounding a major 9th lower than written)
  - Trumpet in D (sounding a tone higher than written)
  - Bass trumpet in E♭ (sounding a major 6th lower than written)
  - Tenor tuba in B♭ (sounding a tone lower than written)
  - Contrabassoon and double bass (sounding an octave lower than written).

Sonority

- The instrumentation ranges from the use of a limited number of instruments through to tutti, though in the prescribed sections full tutti is only rarely used
- The introductory 'dudki' section is scored mainly for wind instruments
- The work opens with a very high unaccompanied solo for bassoon

- Other woodwind effects include
  - Tremolandi in flutes (Fig. 7)
  - Flutter-tonguing in flute, oboes and clarinets (Fig. 10)
- Strings play a minor role, their involvement being limited to:
  - Pizzicato violin and viola (Fig. 4)
  - Violin trill (Fig. 6)
  - Pizzicato solo cello (Fig. 7)
  - Single sustained bass note on solo double bass (Fig. 8)
  - Divisi double basses, four playing harmonics, one muted, one playing pizzicato with two muted cellos (Fig. 10)
  - Glissandi harmonics effect on violas (Fig. 11)
- 'The Augurs of Spring' contains the celebrated stamping chords (Fig. 13) with eight-part string chords formed from four sets of double-stopping (i.e. violin II, viola, cello and bass)
- Each chord is heavily accented (down bows), and reinforced by intermittent doubling by eight horns
- The passage at Fig. 14 is lightly scored for cor anglais, bassoons and pizzicato cellos
- Other effects in this section include:
  - Muted trumpet chords followed by flutter-tonguing in flutes and clarinets (Figs. 16–17)
  - *Col legno* (wood of the bow) at Fig. 24 combined with tremolandi in bassoons and violins
  - The background texture at Figs. 28–29, involving trills in clarinets and bassoons, ostinato in trombone, flute melody, string scales, triangle and antique cymbals, overlaid by the trumpets in parallel chords
  - Tremolo harmonics in violin I at Figs. 33–34
  - Horn glissandi at Fig. 36
- In 'Ritual of Abduction', horns play *bouché* (hand-stopped) accented notes (Fig. 40).

Texture

Textures are many and varied.

In the Introduction, notice particularly:

- The monophonic opening, followed by a passage for two parts at bars 2–3
- Three parts forming a sort of melody and accompaniment at Fig. 1
- The 'layered' texture at Fig. 4
- Four-part (legato) homorhythms at the fifth bar after Fig. 6.

In 'The Augurs of Spring', notice:

- Homorhythmic chords (Fig. 13)
- Ostinato with broken chord support (Fig. 14)
- Melody-dominated homophony with melodic fragments heard over repeated chords (Fig. 15)
- Cross-rhythmic layers (Fig. 16) of ostinato in straight quavers with triplet quavers in violas, overlaid with chordal blasts and brief melodic snatches
- Brief canonic entries (Figs. 20–21)
- Melody-dominated homophony, with multi-layered accompaniment (Fig. 25)

'Ritual of Abduction' contains an almost full homophonic tutti (Figs. 43–44).

Dynamics

- The dynamic range of the first three sections of *The Rite of Spring* covers the full range *pp* - *ff* (the first *fff* and *ppp* do not occur until later in the work)
- No dynamic level is given for the bassoon solo, either at the opening or on its return at Fig. 12; evidently this aspect was left to the discretion of the instrumentalist and conductor.

Tempo, metre and rhythm

- Celebrated for its rhythmic complexity, especially in the final dance with constantly shifting metres
- The Introduction contrasts with the remaining prescribed passages because of its slow rubato tempo (*Lento tempo rubato*) at the start
- Notice the frequent changes of time signature and tempo (e.g. *poco accelerando*, *più mosso*)
- 'The Augurs of Spring' (Fig. 13) is:
  - *Tempo giusto* (strict time)
  - Duple time
  - With frequent asymmetric stresses, i.e. stresses which occur at irregular intervals
  - Pulse is relentless apart from two pause bars before Fig. 22
  - There are also two triple time bars before Fig. 28
- 'Ritual of Abduction' is *presto* with frequent metrical irregularities:
  - The opening in $\frac{9}{8}$ is sometimes subdivided into $\frac{4}{8}$ + $\frac{5}{8}$ (Figs 39 and 41)
  - Time signatures change rapidly from Fig. 42 ($\frac{6}{8}, \frac{7}{8}, \frac{5}{8}$)
  - Melody at Fig. 47 is variously stressed in either $\frac{6}{8}$ or $\frac{3}{4}$
- **Rhythms** range from quavers and semiquavers (Figs. 14 and 25) to:

- Subdivisions of the beat into triplets (Fig. 3), sextuplets (Fig. 4), septuplets (Fig. 10) and groups of 10 (Fig. 9)
- Cross-rhythms, e.g. eight demi-semiquavers against six semiquavers (Fig. 5), four semiquavers against three quavers (Fig. 7) and 3s against 2s (Fig. 16)
- Off-beat stress, e.g. 'straight' off-beat quavers at third bar of Fig. 31, and the asymmetric accents at Fig. 13
- Regular displaced stress at Fig. 40, with every fourth quaver in $\frac{9}{8}$ accented
- Scotch snap, e.g. 2 bars after Fig. 9 in piccolo clarinet
- Syncopation, e.g. Fig. 32, bass line.

Melody

- Stravinsky's earliest works draw extensively on folk music
- In *The Rite*, he drew heavily on a collection of Lithuanian (NB not Russian) folk songs, edited by Anton Juszkiewicz and published in Poland in 1900 as *Litauische Volks-Weisen*
- Perhaps Lithuanian folk song was selected because paganism persisted longer in Lithuania than in Russia itself
- The famous opening theme of *The Rite* was derived from No. 157 of the Juszkiewicz collection, the original four metrically regular triple-time phrases transformed into an improvisatory line:

Bassoon

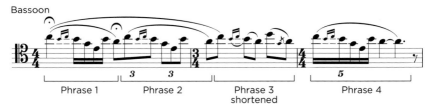

Phrase 1   Phrase 2   Phrase 3 shortened   Phrase 4

- Notice the following features showing folksong influences:
  - Grace notes
  - Hexatonic (six-note) scale, an extension of the pentatonic scale
- The melody three bars after Fig. 37 in the 'Ritual of Abduction' is another borrowing from Juszkiewicz:

(a)   (b)   (c)   (d)

- Pitch outline has been preserved almost intact, but
- The time signature has been changed from $\frac{2}{4}$ to $\frac{9}{8}$
- The last two phrases are separated by a rest

- Further evidence of folk influences can be found in motifs with limited ranges, e.g. Fig. 2:

Other characteristic features of the melodic writing include:

- Chromatic lines, e.g. Fig. 4 in the piccolo clarinet
- Wide leaps, e.g. Fig. 8 in flute
- Angular lines, involving 4ths and 5ths, e.g. Fig. 9 in oboe:

- Ostinati, e.g. the four-note figure which runs throughout the 'The Augurs of Spring' after first appearing in violin I, four bars after Fig. 12:

- Repeated note figures and conjunct lines, e.g. fifth bar of Fig. 28:

- Breaking down and reforming of melodic lines, e.g. Fig. 25 where fragments of the first four bars are reworked in the second four-bar phrase:

- Whooping hunting calls (perfect 5ths) at Fig. 40 in 'Ritual of Abduction'.

Harmony

- Non-functional (i.e. avoidance of cadential harmony)
- Dissonant
- Drones (e.g. Fig. 24)
- Ostinati (Fig. 28 in double bass and cellos)
- Harmonic stasis (e.g. Fig. 13)
- Parallelism:
    - 4ths (Fig. 1 in clarinets)
    - Parallel 4ths and 7ths (Fig. 3 in bassoons)
- Whole-tone structures, e.g. the chord of B♭–D–E–G♯, albeit clouded by chromatic movement, at Fig. 8
- Bitonal structures, e.g. Fig. 13 with its combination of F♭ major (enharmonic E major) in the bass and dominant 7th of A♭ in treble:

- Polytonal structures, e.g. Fig. 14 with chords of E major, E minor, C major and V⁷ of A♭
- Superimposed 5ths chord (E♭–B♭–F–C–G–D), combined with C major broken chord (Fig. 16)
- Superimposed 4ths chord (one beat before Fig. 18)
- Parallel second inversion 7th chords, embedded in the middle of an opulent orchestral texture (Fig. 28) – see example from Fig. 28 on page 139
- Parallel 7th chords, again as part of a larger texture
- Dissonances involving 9th chords (Fig. 37).

Structure and tonality

- The music is organised in 'blocks' of sound, sometimes internally organised as a sort of mosaic made up of short contrasting fragments
- There are vestigial tonal references (drones and melodies), but avoidance of functional tonality
- Some landmarks are given in the table:

Reference point	'Tonality'	Content
Figs. 1–13		**Introduction**
Bars 1–3	Hexatonic on A: notice the major-minor ambiguity	(a) Lithuanian folk-song (see page 138) – chromatic continuation – Lithuanian folk-song reprised
Figs. 2–4	C$\sharp$	(b) Cor anglais melody (see page 139)
Figs 4–6	E major background	(c) Chromatic line
Figs. 6–8	Moving to region of B$\flat$	(b) varied with continuation – (c)–(b)–(c)–(b)–(c)
Fig. 9	F mixolydian in oboe and piccolo clarinet	(d) Angular woodwind melodies (see page 139)
Fig. 10	E major/minor^7 background to polytonal winds	(b), (c) and (d) combined
Fig. 12	A$\flat$ minor	(a) reprised a semitone lower than at the opening; first appearance of the four-note ostinato (see page 139)
Figs. 13–37		**'The Augurs of Spring' ('Les augures printaniers')**
Figs. 13–14	Bitonal (F$\flat$ major + V^7 of A$\flat$) – polytonal – bitonal	Stamping chords
Fig. 15	Bitonal	Chords plus conjunct melodic fragment (e)

Figs. 16–17	Bitonal – E♭ + C + V⁷ of A♭	Ostinato with (e) varied
Figs. 18–22	Bitonal	Chords plus melody involving repeated notes and conjunct movement (f), eventually treated canonically
Figs. 22–24	Moving to modal C	Ostinato
Fig. 25	C mixolydian	New folk-like melody (g – see page 139) plus C pedal and ostinato with (e) at Fig. 26
Fig. 27	E♭ mixolydian	(g) varied on alto flute
Figs. 28–30	E♭ mixolydian expanded through addition of G♭s in strings	(g) varied and continued + (h – see page 139)
Fig. 31	Expanded D	(g) fragmented
Fig. 32	Expanded C – with bass syncopated ostinato gravitating to dominant	(g) fragmented
Figs. 37–47		**'Ritual of Abduction' ('Jeu du rapt')**
Figs. 37–40	Melody on A mixolydian, with bitonal support (V⁷ of A♭ + C)	Second Lithuanian folk song (I – see page 138)
Figs. 40–41	Horn 5ths (A–D) alternating with melody in B♭	Horn call (j); (i)

Fig. 42	Polytonal, involving E♭, F#7, C and a diminished 7th	
Fig. 43	Expanded F#, down-shifted to expanded F	Contrasting material (k); mainly stepwise movement harmonised in block chords
Fig. 44	V7 of B♭, with horns on D	
Fig. 46	On F	(i) fragmented
Fig. 47	F major/minor; concludes with E♭ trill linking with 'Spring Rounds' section	(i) fragmented and punctuated by chords

FURTHER LISTENING

- Listen to Stravinsky's own interpretation of *The Rite of Spring*, dating from 1960 (Sony BMG Music Entertainment label)
- Other nationalist works by Stravinsky:
  - *The Firebird*
  - *Petrouchka*
  - *Les Noces (The Wedding)*
- Other contemporary works:
  - Ravel: *Daphnis et Chloé*
  - Debussy: *Jeux*
  - Bartók: *The Miraculous Mandarin.*

Sample materials for Question 6 (Section B, essay 2)

This chapter provides examples of the types of question normally set for Section B, essay 2. You may find it helpful to bear in mind the following points:

1. The Specification and Edexcel's Sample Assessment Materials (SAMs) state two assessment objectives:

   ■ The demonstration and application of musical knowledge (Assessment Objective 3 **[AO3]**)

   ■ The use of analytical and appraising skills leading to evaluation and critical judgement about the work in question (Assessment Objective 4 **[AO4]**).

   The other assessment objectives concern performance issues (AO1) and composition skills (AO2).

2. There will be three questions on the exam paper: you choose **one** to answer.

3. You will have a good idea what to expect before going into the exam room, as the essay questions are distinctly formulaic. All the essays in the SAMs open with the command word 'evaluate', before going on to name the aspects of the work on which you should focus (for A Level typically three out of structure, tonality, metre, rhythm, melody, harmony, texture, sonority or instrumentation, technology, etc.). You are also requested to relate your discussion to other relevant works.

4. The command words relevant to this type of question are:

   ■ **Evaluate** – make judgements about the stipulated elements and go on to draw conclusions

   ■ **Analyse** – investigate and pick out musical features and show how these features contribute to the effect created

   ■ **Discuss** – this may involve setting out the issues raised by the question; considering the various aspects arising in the course of the investigation; and applying a reasoned approach in the presentation of the response.

5. At A Level there are 30 marks for this question: 10 marks for AO3 and 20 marks for AO4.

6. The final mark is awarded on the basis of a 'general impression', rather than the awarding of marks for individual comments. The mark schemes that follow show how this system could operate in practice. As a first step, compare the following statements concerning the first movement of *Symphonie fantastique* by Berlioz:

'A pedal occurs at bars 46-59.'

'A pedal occurs at bars 46-59 which, unlike the more usual goal-oriented pedals of Baroque and Classical music, is used to support a number of different keys (Db, E major, C# minor, G# minor, etc), underlining the dreamy qualities of the music at this point.'

The first statement is accurate and would be credited under AO3. The second statement is not only worthy of credit under AO3, but in assessing its expressive effect in relation to the work's programme it also qualifies for credit under AO4.

> See the grid provided in the SAM Mark Scheme for details of the five levels that examiners will consider in scoring the final mark. The lowest level (Marks 1–6) refers to 'limited awareness of contextual factors', 'little reference to texts', 'limited organisation of ideas', 'some basic musical vocabulary used with errors/inconsistency' and 'little attempt to link to other relevant works'. In contrast, the top level (Marks 25–30) will be awarded to candidates who make 'sophisticated links between the music and its historical, social and cultural context', who offer 'a critical evaluative argument with sustained musical examples', make good use of terminology and make reference to 'relevant works... to justify points'.

7. Your answers in this section should be in continuous prose. If you write in note form or use bullet points, you will not be awarded marks in the highest band. On the other hand, if you are running out of time, it would still be sensible to offer information in note form, providing that your notes are clear.

8. Finally, remember that you will be provided with a resources booklet, which contains representative extracts from the works in question. You will not have access to the complete Anthology, so you must develop a good overall

grasp of the prescribed works by way of preparation and be able to find ways of locating devices and various sections without necessarily using bar numbers.

For more practice with Question 6, see Rhinegold Education's *Edexcel AS and A Level Music Study Guide* (RHG341), which contains a practice question for each set work, along with guidance on how to structure your answers.

Read the following questions carefully so that you are sure about the sort of information you are required to produce. If you are uncertain about what is meant, refer to the terminology section earlier in the book.

Vocal music

Evaluate Vaughan Williams' use of sonority, melody and harmony in 'Bredon Hill' in conveying the sense of Housman's text.

Relate your discussion to other relevant works. These may include set works, wider listening or other music.

Mark scheme

Before studying the mark scheme (indicative content) below, attempt the question yourself. You will find it useful to compare your answer with the mark scheme and the sample answer that follows.

The expression 'indicative content' used by examination boards simply refers to the sort of information that examiners look for when marking students' exam papers.

Indicative content

Answers should show a greater emphasis on analysis, evaluation and forming of judgements, rather than the simple statement of facts.

Sonority

Scored for tenor, piano and strings, often using high ranges through the use of harmonics. **[AO3]**

- **String techniques include:**
  - Pizzicato in violin I only (bars 100–109) **[AO3]** to reinforce the effect of the tolling funeral bell **[AO4]**
  - Mutes in all instruments **[AO3]**
  - Double-stopping **[AO3]**
  - Tremolo (e.g. bars 123–130) **[AO3]** to underline distraught feelings **[AO4]**
  - Down bows for emphasis (violin II and viola, bar 128) **[AO3]** to emphasise the anger of the protagonist **[AO4]**
- **Piano:**
  - Passage for just the piano accompanying voice (bars 52-83) **[AO3]** makes the situation more immediate (in contrast with earlier ethereal string writing) **[AO4]**
  - Triplet parallel 5th and octave chords **[AO3]** for pealing bell effects **[AO4]**
  - Extensive use of both *una corda* and sustaining pedal simultaneously (e.g. opening) **[AO3]** creating sense of distance and space **[AO4]**
  - Use of tremolo **[AO3]** underlying distraught emotions. **[AO4]**

Melody

- Word-setting is mainly syllabic, with the occasional slurrings **[AO3]**
- Melisma is used for special emphasis **[AO3]**, e.g. 'pray' **[AO4]**
- The melody is in G pentatonic major at the outset, but the wider range of notes results in mixolydian mode and then aeolian mode **[AO3]**, the uncomplicated folk element hinting at an idyllic pastoral scene **[AO4]**
- Mainly step movement, with occasional leaps **[AO3]**
- Span of melody narrows **[AO3]** for the 'funeral' music **[AO4]**
- Chromaticism **[AO3]** intensifies sombre mood **[AO4]**

- The funereal mood is further intensified by a line in the piano, largely restricted to an interval of a 2nd **[AO3 and 4]**
- The repeated descending triplet in piano and strings **[AO3]** is an angry response to the 'noisy bells'. **[AO4]**

Harmony

- Use of 7th chords, which when superimposed result in chords of an 11th **[AO3]**
- Colouristic overlapping parallel 4ths **[AO3]** simulating bells **[AO4]**
- 7ths are sometimes inverted **[AO3]**
- Static or slow-moving progressions **[AO3]** help portray the open landscape **[AO4]**
- Tension heightened (at bar 84) **[AO4]** when the A♮ becomes an A♭ **[AO3]**
- Bitonal structures based on A♭ and G **[AO3]** intensify the drama of the situation. **[AO4]**

Reference could usefully be made to contemporary works by e.g. Ravel, Schoenberg, Strauss, etc.

Sample answer

Mark this answer yourself, commenting on its good points and whether these satisfy AO3, AO4 or both. In addition, make a note of any aspects which could have been improved. Check your assessment against the examiner's comments that follow, after completing your marking.

In his setting of 'Bredon Hill', Vaughan Williams has to move from the idyllic scene on Bredon Hill of two lovers on a summertime Sunday morning to the wintertime funeral of the girl. Throughout bells play an important role in both the imagery of the poem and aspects of the musical setting.

The calm pastoral scene is immediately set with bell-like 7th chords on high muted strings and lower-placed chords on piano. The piano also includes bell-like parallel 4ths, perhaps reminiscent of the bell sonorities of Ravel's piano piece, 'La Vallée des Cloches' from the cycle 'Miroirs'. The harmony here is also similar to that of the French impressionist composers, which may well be a result of Vaughan Williams' time in France the preceding year, during which period he took lessons from Ravel.

The harmonic scheme is often slow-moving, and in fact the voice enters against the background of a static 11th chord. The vocal line at first has a folksong-like feel to it. With a key signature of G major, it is pentatonic for the first few bars, later broadening to take in a mixolydian F natural and, at the end of the stanza, a minor mode inflection of a Bb. After a second verse, treated in a similar way, the calm of the opening is gradually undermined. The piano alone accompanies the voice in this section, and introduces an insistent peal of bells effect (parallel 5ths and 8ths) in the right hand with chords in the left hand, sometimes 7ths which are inverted on occasion. The vocal line gradually becomes more complex with a widening of range and introduction of melismas (on 'people' and 'pray').

The funereal section of the songs is introduced by a darkening of the harmony by way of chromaticism (the section marked più lento). When the voice enters, the three upper strings sustain an open 5ths chord (G-D-G) with chilling effect while the piano adds an Ab below. Partway through the stanza, the vocal line rises from G into the region of Bb minor, and is supported by strings playing common chords moving in parallel. The vocal line itself is almost entirely conjunct and involves inversions of itself as well as increased amounts of chromaticism.

A sort of funeral march is heard, and here Vaughan Williams simulates the effect of the single tolling bell with octave Gs on piano, reinforced by bowed G octaves on violin II and pizzicato octave Gs on violin I. In addition, there are tolling 7th chords in the piano left hand and an insistent two-chord figure in the right hand of stepwise parallel 5ths and 8ths. The vocal line is in minor mode and retains a folk-like sound with a modal flattened 7th (F natural).

The final stage of the setting provides further evidence of impressionist influences, the stringed instruments (now unmuted) play long-held harmonies, while the pianist plays rippling 7th chords with both pedals applied to produce a hazy effect. This is a little like another piece by Ravel, 'Une Barque sur l'océan', but it must be said that it is rather less involved. The vocal line at first repeats the melody of the first stanza, but the man's exasperation at being pursued by the sound of the 'noisy bells' leads to his climactic outburst, touching on a high A before a descent to the tonic G which takes in some chromatic writing. This passage is deliberately sung in free time, independently of the accompaniment with its tremolandi and savage down-bowed triplets combined with ostinato on piano (right hand). The song ends with the sonorities and chord structures heard at the opening and the singer's last three words: 'I will come'.

'Bredon Hill' is an effective setting, both in the way it sets the scene and relays the narrative. Vaughan Williams' style reveals both his liking for English folk music and an awareness of some more recent developments in European music, though stopping short at the avant-garde approach to word-setting evident in e.g. Schoenberg's 'Pierrot Lunaire' (Sprechgesang) and the extreme dissonance levels of much contemporary music of the time.

Examiner's points

This is basically a sound account of the content of 'Bredon Hill' which keeps to the brief and provides both accurate descriptions of the song's content and the ways in which the content of the text is conveyed.

There are useful references to music which was composed almost contemporaneously, especially the works by Ravel. It might have been possible, however, to explore the social and cultural context at greater depth, so this essay probably hovers at the upper end of Level 4.

Instrumental music

Evaluate Berlioz's use of melody, harmony and tonality in *Symphonie fantastique*, movement I, bars 1-64, to convey the 'dreamy melancholy' mentioned in the programme.

Relate your discussion to other relevant works. These may include set works, wider listening or other music.

Mark scheme

Before studying the mark scheme (indicative content) below, attempt the question yourself. You will find it useful to compare your answer with the mark scheme and the sample answer that follows.

Indicative content

Answers should show a greater emphasis on analysis, evaluation and forming of judgements, rather than the simple statement of facts.

Melody

- The first theme (bar 3) is taken from an early work, the melody taken from *Estelle et Némorin* **[AO3]**
- The following features portray a free play of thought **[AO4]**:
  - The fluctuations between stepwise movement and leaps (variously minor 6th, perfect 4th, octave and 3rds) **[AO3]**
  - Fluidity arising from frequent rests and pauses
  - Appoggiaturas also indicate melancholy. **[AO4]**

Harmony

- Functional harmony, with a strong drive to cadences **[AO3]**, especially imperfect, hinting at continually unfolding day-dreams **[AO4]**
- Some chords are expressive of melancholy **[AO4]**:
  - Diminished 7th (bar 3, beat 3, reinforced by appoggiatura)
  - 'Neapolitan' D♭ at bar 42

- Pedals on A♭ from bars 46-59 **[AO3]**, the wide range of chords supported indicating a wandering mind **[AO4]**:

  - Diminished 7th (bar 46)

  - D♭ chord (bar 49)

  - E major, with the A♭ regarded as the enharmonic G♯ (bar 53)

  - C♯ minor (bar 55)

  - G♯ minor (bar 57)

  - Diminished 7th again (bar 59)

- Free use of 7ths and 9ths (bar 10) **[AO3]**, where the dissonance is further intensified by the suspended C (11th) to produce poignant effect. **[AO4]**

Tonality

- C minor **[AO3]**

- Avoidance of strong tonic statements **[AO3]** hints at dreaminess **[AO4]**

- Fluid, brief modulations **[AO3]** also hint at dreaminess **[AO4]**

- Pedal supporting chords in many, sometimes remote, tonalities **[AO3]** indicates dreaminess.

Sample answer

Mark this answer yourself, commenting on its good points and whether these satisfy AO3, AO4 or both. In addition, make a note of any aspects which could have been improved.

Check your assessment against the examiner's comments that follow, after completing your marking.

Bars 1-64 of the first movement of Berlioz's 'Symphonie fantastique' form a slow introduction to the main part of the movement, and are dominated by a mood of melancholy. It matches Berlioz's programme admirably, even though it was mainly lifted from an early work – 'Estelle et Némorin' – composed many years before in Berlioz's early teens, and the 'Rêveries' announced in the movement's title are mirrored in the changes of tempo and shifting tonalities.

Cast in the key of C minor, the opening section begins with two introductory bars for woodwind and horns. The first main theme, heard on muted strings, consists of a series of fragmentary phrases of varying lengths and involves no repetition of patterns, e.g. the first phrase, marked by dotted rhythm, step-wise movement and appoggiaturas, is answered by a series of breathless fragments involving some leaps. The harmony here is immediately arresting with a secondary dominant, preceded by a diminished 7th, at the end of the first phrase, while the three remaining phrases all move to the dominant, the last time a dominant 9th. There is some chromatic movement in the inner parts.

This is followed by two two-bar phrases, the second a modified repeat of the first. Each phrase opens with an octave leap, and diminished 7ths are prominent. The first phrase moves to Eb major, and the second finishes on an Eb chord with Db (7th). The final stage of this opening melody features further brief fragments with appoggiaturas and seems to peter out inconclusively on a sustained G in bass.

At this point the pace picks up and in fact the sustained G in the bass leads to a perfect cadence in C major. Here there is a lively scalic line in violins. In fact, this apparently new departure proves to be short-lived because Berlioz steers the music round to C minor and a return to the slower opening tempo. There are clear references to the triplets of the introduction before the reappearance of the main theme, this time re-harmonised and much more richly scored. This harmonisation leads much more in the direction of Eb major, and it is only halfway through the varied repetition that the key returns to C minor. The final section is also extended, and after incorporating a 'Neapolitan' Db chord, eventually ends with an interrupted cadence to mark the start of one of the most ingenious portions of the introduction.

The interrupted cadence comes to rest on a diminished 7th chord with Ab in the bass. The Ab becomes a pedal underpinning a number of references to distant keys. The diminished 7th resolves on Ab and is followed by a Db chord supporting a descending conjunct melody on horn and broken chord patterns on violins. The key also passes to E major, then C# minor and G# minor. Finally, a more conventional chord progression signals the move to the key of C major, the chords here being A minor (VI), D minor first inversion (IIb) leading to Ic, V7 and I (C major).

This symphony was truly epoch-making and marked a new departure in Romantic musical thinking. There had been a number of programmatic symphonies prior to this work, going right back to Haydn ('Le Matin' and 'Lamentatione') and Beethoven ('Pastoral'). Mendelssohn, working contemporaneously with Berlioz also produced loosely programmatic works (e.g. 'Scotch' and 'Italian'), but Berlioz was the first to produce an autobiographical work, placing his own feelings and emotions centre-stage. Arguably, it was not an achievement which was repeated until Richard Strauss's 'Ein Heldenleben' and 'Sinfonia Domestica'.

Examiner's points

The writer framed this response successfully with both introductory remarks establishing the source of this particular part of the symphony, and a conclusion which cited other relevant examples of programmatic writing.

Throughout, there were sound musical observations under AO3, and devices were successfully located. There could have been more explicit attempts to relate such devices to the 'dreamy melancholy' mentioned in the question, but this generally successful response would perhaps gain a mark at the upper end of the Level 4 band.

Music for film

> Evaluate Herrmann's use of rhythm and metre, sonority and texture in *Psycho* 'The Toys', 'The Cellar' and 'Finale', showing how these elements contribute to the creation of an appropriate underscore.
>
> Relate your discussion to other relevant works. These may include set works, wider listening or other music.

Mark scheme

Before studying the mark scheme (indicative content) below, attempt the question yourself. You will find it useful to compare your answer with the mark scheme and the sample answer that follows.

Indicative content

Answers should show a greater emphasis on analysis, evaluation and forming of judgements, rather than the simple statement of facts.

Some contextual information should be provided, showing why this film and its score are so celebrated. **[AO4]**

Rhythm and metre

- Fast-paced, duple time in 'The Cellar' (Allegro molto) **[AO3]**, heightening sensation of fear **[AO4]**
- 'The Toys' is in slow quadruple time **[AO3]**
- The slow 'Finale' music alternates between quadruple and triple time **[AO3]** perhaps underlining the strangeness of the situation **[AO4]**
- Other notable features **[AO3]** include:
  - Constant, hard-driven quavers ('The Cellar') for frantic feel **[AO4]**
  - Steadily moving crotchets ('The Toys')
  - Syncopation ('Finale', viola at bars 12-14).

Sonority

- Muted strings are used in all three of the prescribed cues **[AO3]**
- Numerous performing techniques **[AO3]** are used for variety and expressive force **[AO4** for explanations]:
  - Repeated down bows ('The Toys')
  - Combinations of arco and pizzicato ('The Toys')
  - Tremolandi (on divisi strings) ('The Cellar')
  - Sul ponticello ('The Cellar')
  - Relatively high lines ('Finale')

Texture

[AO3] for the following observations and **[AO4]** for valid comments on their effect:

- Homophony ('The Toys')
- Pedal ('The Toys')
- Varying densities:
  - Monophony ('Finale', bars 1-3)
  - Two-part ('Finale', bars 1-11)
  - Three-part ('Finale', bars 12 onwards)
  - Four-part divisi in both violin I and II ('The Toys')
- Octaves ('The Cellar', bars 1-4) with trills
- Imitative entries in 'The Cellar' from bar 5, creating a sort of fugal exposition
- Homorhythmic chords ('Finale', bars 18-19)
- Free counterpoint ('Finale', bars 3-17).

Sample answer

Mark this answer yourself, commenting on its good points and whether these satisfy AO3, AO4 or both. In addition, make a note of any aspects which could have been improved. Check your assessment against the examiner's comments that follow, after completing your marking.

Rhythm in 'The Toys' is very simple. There is a steady crotchet rhythm in viola and cello throughout, while double bass has notes lasting almost a whole bar at a time and the upper parts move in minims and semibreves. Muted strings are used, the upper parts divided into four parts.

Texture here is homophonic. The low strings provide pedal notes while the violin I play 7th chords which gradually descend, violin II doubling some but not all of these chords.

'The Cellar' is a fast duple time movement, which after the introductory longer notes (minims and crotchet-quaver patterns) is largely in constant quavers until the final sustained chords (minims tied over several bars).

Like 'The Toys' this movement involves muted strings, but the string writing here includes trills at the start and tremolandos applied throughout the main part of the movement until the final bars.

Texture is more varied here, with octaves to begin with. There is then something rather like a fugue with entries coming in one after another, starting with the lowest and working upwards. It differs from traditional fugues because firstly the subject itself is split up between divided forces with e.g. one group of double basses and cellos playing for one bar, after which the second group plays a bar, and so on. This applies in all sections, i.e. after the double basses and cellos in order of entry, the violas, violin II and violin I. The other difference is that all the entries come in on the same note, i.e. G and in the case of viola, violin II and violin I this is even at the same pitch.

Eventually the four parts reduce to two real parts consisting of a sustained note in the bass and the three upper parts all sharing the same material. This then reduces to a single line which leads into the final chord which is gradually built up from the lowest note.

The 'Finale' is a slow, mainly triple-time movement, although there are some occasional quadruple-time bars. To begin with it moves in a steady crotchet rhythm, latterly incorporating minims and dotted rhythms.

Syncopation occurs part way through and again in the chords at the end.

Sonority is distinctive with almost the whole cue being written for the three uppermost instruments. The writing in fact gets increasingly high until the very end when cello and double bass finally enter and the last chords are heard at a much lower register. Strings are played muted, arco throughout without any other technical devices.

Texture at some points is contrapuntal. It opens with monophony for viola. Violin II enters to create a two-part texture, and three-part counterpoint is heard once violin I enters. Right at the end there is homophony of four-part chords in upper strings supported by sustained bass note.

Examiner's points

This essay included a significant amount of AO3 information regarding all the elements specified in the question. Unfortunately, there was no attempt to provide any contextual information, or include reference to other works. Musical vocabulary is well used, but in the absence of further AO4 commentary, this essay might well be placed in Level 2.

Popular music and jazz

> **Evaluate sonority, melody and structure in 'Eleanor Rigby' and 'Tomorrow Never Knows' from *Revolver*, in order to assess the innovative qualities of the Beatles' contribution to the popular music of the day.**
>
> Relate your discussion to other relevant works. These may include set works, wider listening or other music.

Mark scheme

Before studying the mark scheme (indicative content) below, attempt the question yourself. You will find it useful to compare your answer with the mark scheme and the sample answer that follows.

Indicative content

Answers should show a greater emphasis on analysis, evaluation and forming of judgements, rather than the simple statement of facts.

AO4 credit will be awarded for establishing The Beatles' place in the development of popular music. Reference should be made to the music of other pop composers.

'Eleanor Rigby'

Sonority

- 'Double' string quartet **[AO3]** suggesting sonority of Herrmann's *Psycho* **[AO4]**
- Mechanical staccato figurations **[AO3]** indicates lack of human warmth **[AO4]**
- Performed non-vibrato, and recorded with microphones close to the instruments **[AO3]** also contributing to sense of alienation. **[AO4]**

Melody

- The melody is modally ambiguous, with both lydian and dorian inflections
- Unusual phrase structure of five bars of 1 + 3 + 1 **[AO3]**, used to highlight names of characters, narrative and message **[AO4]**
- Use of sequence **[AO3]**
- Underlying despair **[AO4]** underlined by leaps of octave and minor 10th. **[AO3]**

Structure

- The song is in modified strophic form, with three verses, preceded by an introduction and followed by a chorus **[AO3]**
- Each verse consists of two lines of five bars, followed by a chorus of two four-bar phrases. **[AO3]**

'Tomorrow never knows'

Sonority

- Striking sound arising from studio effects **[AO3]**
- Lennon's vocal part was recorded with automatic double-tracking **[AO3** and **AO4** for explanation of effects]

- Use of revolving Leslie speaker (found in Hammond organs) **[AO3]** to produce effect of chanting Tibetan monks **[AO4]**
- Use of tape loops, freely combined **[AO3]**, including 'seagull' effect (speeded up tape of McCartney), an orchestral chord of B♭ major, an electric guitar phrase, reversed and played at double speed, sitar-like sound, reversed and played at double speed.

Melody

- 4 + 2 + 2 bar phrasing **[AO3]**
- Tonic broken chord at opening **[AO3]** has powerful effect hinting at elemental force **[AO4]**
- The two last phrases move from 5th degree up to flattened 7th and then tonic
- Flattened 3rds can be heard in the tape loops.

Structure and tonality

- The key is C, with prominent flattened 7th (mixolydian) **[AO3]**
- Powerfully direct **[AO4]** strophic structure **[AO3]** consisting of introduction, three verses of eight bars each, instrumental (16 bars), four more verses, coda and outro.

Sample answer

Mark this answer yourself, commenting on its good points and whether these satisfy AO3, AO4 or both. In addition, make a note of any aspects which could have been improved. Check your assessment against the examiner's comments that follow, after completing your marking.

These two numbers are among the most innovative works in the Beatles' output and helped to make 'Revolver' one of the most progressive albums of the day. To a considerable degree, this was due to the contribution of both the album's producer, George Martin, and the recording engineer, Geoff Emerick, who spent 300 hours in the studio perfecting the final sound.

Both the numbers under discussion are notably different in terms of sonority from the standard sound of the day – for examples of that sound, see the other prescribed songs, 'Here, there and everywhere' and 'I want to tell you', where the typical line up consists of vocals, backing vocals, bass and rhythm guitars, percussion and piano. For one thing, none of the typical pop-music instruments are employed in 'Eleanor Rigby', being replaced by eight strings, a sort of doubled string quartet, the incorporation of 'classical' instruments being a characteristic of the Beatles' approach in their later albums. The strings are dry-sounding, the raw quality arising partly from the placing of mics close to the instruments and the performers' aggressive 'staccato' attack. This scoring was in fact the work of George Martin, and it is thought that the approach to the instruments was suggested by Herrmann's writing for strings for the score of 'Psycho' which had been released only a few years before. The performing group is completed by the lead vocal and backing vocals, introduced in the refrain.

'Revolver' marked a significant change in approach as it would not easily be possible to perform some of these numbers 'live', i.e. outside the recording studio. In fact, 'Tomorrow Never Knows' could never be recreated exactly as it appears on the disc in any case as it involved the loose assembling of a number of tape loops, some of which were subject to a distortion to a greater or lesser extent, e.g. loop 2, which is often described as sounding a bit like seagulls but in fact was a speeded-up version of McCartney laughing. Other effects were used: Lennon's voice was distorted by being put through a revolving Leslie speaker to sound like chanting Tibetan monks. Various other sounds are brought in from time to time, e.g. orchestral chords of Bb and C – all arbitrarily mixed together as part of a game of chance.

Melodies are also highly distinctive. Modality was not new in pop music, the aeolian mode being frequently used in Blues songs. In 'Eleanor Rigby', however, the effect is more wide-ranging, with F# over C major chords sounding lydian. The melodic phrasing is also irregular, the verse consisting of 1 + 3 + 1 bars, with the melody making frequent use of sequence, e.g. the descending sequence hinting at the dorian mode with the appearance of C#. Much of the melody here moves by step, though a broken triad appears in the first bar of the vocal, and effective use is made of larger leaps in the chorus, first an octave and then a 10th ('Where do they all come from?').

Melody in the case of 'Tomorrow Never Knows' is much more basic – an eight-bar statement dividing into 4 + 2 + 2 bars. Its most telling aspects are the widely spaced broken chord figures hinting at power and might, and the mixolydian Bb to C.

Structure in 'Eleanor Rigby' is a straightforward strophic design of introduction, verse and chorus repeated three times and postlude. There are slight variations in the instrumental parts, but the song never departs from its basic tonality of E minor, and indeed the restriction of the harmony to two chords (E minor and C major) makes cadential harmony impossible. As already observed, the phrase structure of the verse is irregular (two five-bar phrases), but the chorus is made up of two four-bar phrases. 'Tomorrow' is also largely strophic with introduction, though the design is complicated by the presence of an instrumental, so the final scheme is intro – 3 verses – instrumental – 4 verses – coda and fade-out.

From this point, the Beatles' approach became entirely studio-based, and this enabled them and their producer to create some striking effects, one of the most celebrated being the orchestral links in 'Day in the Life' on 'Sergeant Pepper'. They also paved the way for the so-called ambient approach to be found in such albums as David Bowie's 'Low'.

Examiner's points

This is an effective survey of the two songs. Some limited attempt is made to refer to other albums and artists, although more information would have been welcome. This work might very well be placed at the top end of Level 4.

Fusions

Evaluate Shankar's use of melody, harmony and instrumentation in 'Burn' from *Breathing Under Water*, **showing how a piece of fusion music has been created.**

Relate your discussion to other relevant works. These may include set works, wider listening or other music.

Mark scheme

Before studying the mark scheme (indicative content) below, attempt the question yourself. You will find it useful to compare your answer with the mark scheme and the sample answer that follows.

Indicative content

Answers should show a greater emphasis on analysis, evaluation and forming of judgements, rather than the simple statement of facts.

AO4 credit will be awarded for establishing historical context and stylistic features that indicate that this is an Indian/European fusions work. Other composers or types of music should be mentioned, especially in connection with the use of non-European content.

Melody

Answers here should include references to the sitar, vocals and strings.

- Wide range for **sitar** of G♯ in bass to E an octave and a third above middle C in treble **[AO3]**
- Sitar's melody is in the (Western) key of C♯ minor (with some B♯s) **[AO3]** rather than a scale associated with one of the rags **[AO4]**
- There is much typical ornamentation **[AO3]** indicating Indian elements **[AO4]**:
  - Microtonal slides
  - 'Crushed' notes
  - Mordents of varying durations

- The **lead vocal** range is initially limited to just a 6th (C♯ – A) **[AO3]**
- Intervals are narrower, no larger than a 3rd
- The vocal melody includes a sequence **[AO3]** perhaps more European in content **[AO4]**
- Later a lower part touches on B♯ and an additional line extends up to C♯ **[AO3]**
- **Strings** initially have a range of just C♯ to G♯, extending to A at bar 18 **[AO3]**
- The line starting at bar 18 shares links with the vocal line. **[AO3]**

Harmony

- There is an avoidance of cadential harmony **[AO3]**, but notice the near perfect cadence at bars 73–74 (G♯ (sus4) – C♯ (sus4)/E♯), pointing to European influence **[AO4]**
- Harmonic language tends more to European approaches **[AO3]** although the harmonic rhythm is slow, perhaps more reminiscent of Indian music **[AO4]**
- Often quietly dissonant language
- Root position chords (bar 87)
- Sus chords
- Slash chords, some resulting in inversions (e.g. second inversion in bar 9)
- Added note chords (e.g. bar 6)
- Relatively frequent A⁷ – C♯ progression
- C♯ is present throughout, but at bar 22 takes the form of a tonic pedal, a device common to both European and Indian music. **[AO4]**

Instrumentation

- The basic soundworld consists of strings, sitar and vocals **[AO3]**, fusing European and Indian resources **[AO4]**
- A sarangi is introduced in bars 46–53 and sitar is used almost throughout **[AO3]**; additional **[AO4]** credit for explaining characteristic timbral qualities
- Orchestral (European) additions include brass (bar 94), harp (bar 102), flute (bar 104) and cello (bar 107)
- Percussion instruments include a mix of European and Indian instruments:

- Bass drum (bar 14)
- Manjira (hand cymbals) (bar 22)
- Drum kit (bar 22)
- Ride cymbal (bar 29)

Sample answer

Mark this answer yourself, commenting on its good points and whether these satisfy AO3, AO4 or both. In addition, make a note of any aspects which could have been improved. Check your assessment against the examiner's comments that follow, after completing your marking.

It is clear, just from the sound, that 'Bum' is a fusions work combining Indian elements with a Westernised approach, typical of much 'Bollywood' music. The forces required are vocals, 'European' strings and other Western instruments, such as brass, flute, harp and, at the end, a cello solo. The percussion section is also more 'Western pop' with drum kit, bass drum and ride cymbal, but an Indian feature is evident with the use of manjira or hand cymbals. The most obvious Indian features, however, are provided by two instruments in particular, the sitar, a long-necked plucked string instrument with a set of sympathetic strings resonating with the six or seven main strings to produce the unmistakably Indian sound. The other instrument is the sarangi – a bowed instrument with three main strings with as many as 36 sympathetic strings.

Consideration of the melodic element takes in sitar, voice and accompanying strings. The range of the sitar in 'Bum' is wide, covering almost four octaves, and it is a sign of a fusion with Western music that instead of using one of the traditional rags it is largely in C# minor. Indian elements are clear in the ornamentation, notably the slides, crushed notes and mordent-like flourishes.

The range of the vocal line is much narrower as it spans only a 6th, from C# to A, at first. Eventually additional vocal lines reach down to B# and up to C#. There are many repeated notes and step movement, and in fact there are no leaps greater than a 3rd, as can be seen in the descending sequence (G-A-F; F-G-E) on 'every moon' and 'precious kiss'. It should be noted that this sequence is partially disguised as rhythms are varied. The final 'dance with me' also outlines a minor 3rd.

Finally the strings: they too have a limited range of a 6th and also incorporate sequence-like patterns, possibly relating to the vocal line.

Although 'Burn' is clearly in the key of C# minor, with aeolian inflections, the harmony does not really contribute to the underlining of this key through cadential harmony. Instead, the note C# is present in various guises throughout the piece, and in fact appears in the form of a tonic pedal at one point. In spite of the surface liveliness of the melodic lines, the rate of chord change is slow. The harmonies used are often dissonant with added notes, and there is a frequent A7 to tonic progression.

The fact that it is possible to speak of harmonic progressions at all really points to a Western style of writing, as much Indian music is based on drones (see 'Rag Bhairav' in the previous Anthology). Melody, as has been shown, is a sort of mixture of Indian and Western music, with European scales but microtonal ornaments, while the instrumentation also is a combination of the two elements. The end result is typical of much popular Indian music of the present day aimed at a worldwide audience, with the use of modern technology and a fusion style that is reminiscent of the 'Bollywood' idiom.

Examiner's points

This essay covers the main points satisfactorily, although the references to other musical works were slight and generalised. It might well be considered to be on the borderline between Levels 3 and 4.

New directions

Evaluate Stravinsky's use of rhythm, melody and harmony in the prescribed sections from *The Rite of Spring* in relation to other 19th and early 20th century nationalist works.

Relate your discussion to other relevant works. These may include set works, wider listening or other music.

Mark scheme

Before studying the mark scheme (indicative content) below, attempt the question yourself. You will find it useful to compare your answer with the mark scheme and the sample answer that follows.

Indicative content

Answers should show a greater emphasis on analysis, evaluation and forming of judgements, rather than the simple statement of facts.

Credit will be awarded for establishing historical context, circumstances of composition and specific stylistic features that indicate that this work was by Stravinsky. Other nationalist works by contemporary or earlier composers, as well as by Stravinsky himself, should be mentioned. **[AO3/4]**

Rhythm

- Famed for its rhythmic complexity **[AO3]**
- The Introduction contrasts with the remaining prescribed passages with its slow rubato tempo (*Lento tempo rubato*) **[AO3/4]**
- There are frequent changes of time signature and tempo **[AO3]**
- 'The Augurs of Spring' (Fig. 13) is in strict *tempo giusto* duple time **[AO3]** creating a primitive atmosphere **[AO4]**
- There are frequent asymmetric stresses **[AO3]**
- 'Ritual of Abduction' is *presto* with frequent metrical irregularities **[AO3]**
- Typical rhythmic features include subdivisions of the beat into triplets, sextuplets, etc. as well as cross-rhythms, off-beat stresses, scotch snap and syncopation. **[AO3]**

Melody

- In *The Rite*, Stravinsky drew heavily on Lithuanian folk songs **[AO3]**, perhaps because paganism persisted longer in Lithuania than in Russia itself **[AO4]**
- The famous opening theme of *The Rite* was based on a theme of four metrically regular triple-time phrases transformed into an improvisatory line **[AO3/4]**
- Typical folksong features include grace notes and use of hexatonic (six-note) scale, an extension of the pentatonic scale **[AO3]**
- The melody three bars after Fig. 37 in the 'Ritual of Abduction' is another Lithuanian theme **[AO3** with **AO4** credit for commentary**]**
- Many motifs have a limited range, characteristic of folk music **[AO3/4]**
- Typical features include repeated-note figures and step-wise movement **[AO3]**
- Some melodies fragment and reform basic material **[AO3** with **AO4** credit for commentary**]**
- Hunting calls (perfect 5ths) occur in 'Ritual of Abduction' **[AO3]** with primitive effect. **[AO4]**

Harmony

- Non-functional (i.e. avoidance of cadential harmony)
- Dissonant
- Drones
- Ostinati
- Harmonic stasis
- Parallelism
- Whole-tone structures
- Bitonal structures
- Polytonal structures
- Superimposed 5ths chord

All these features contribute to the creation of a primitive, violent sound **[AO4]**

Sample answer

Mark this answer yourself, commenting on its good points and whether these satisfy AO3, AO4 or both. In addition, make a note of any aspects which could have been improved. Check your assessment against the examiner's comments that follow, after completing your marking.

Throughout the 19th century there had been increasing interest in folk music as a source of musical inspiration. Sometimes this arose in connection with political events, as may have been the case with Chopin. In other cases it was also a means of preserving the musical heritage of a nation, for example, the many Norwegian folksongs arranged by Grieg. In Russia, most composers drew on folk music, notably Tchaikovsky (see 'Serenade for Strings' and the finale of Symphony No. 4) and composers of 'The Five', based in St Petersburg, that is Balakirev, Borodin, Cui, Mussorgsky and Rimsky-Korsakov. Rimsky-Korsakov was Stravinsky's teacher and it is undoubtedly the case that it was from Rimsky that he inherited his musically nationalistic attitude, evident in most of his early works. Folk music appears in the two earlier ballets, 'The Firebird' and 'Petrouchka', where there are many literal quotations, e.g. the 'Khorovod' from 'The Firebird' and the 'Wetnurses dance' in the final tableau of 'Petrouchka'. In 'The Rite', however, a very different approach was adopted in that the basic folk material was subject to ingenious transformations of both melodic outline and rhythm.

This process can be seen in the famous bassoon solo right at the opening. Interestingly the melody comes from a collection of Lithuanian folk tunes, 'Litauische Volks-Weisen', edited by Anton Juszkiewicz and published in Kraków (Poland) in 1900. The use of Lithuanian rather than Russian material was never properly explained, but it may have been because pagan practices persisted in Lithuania much longer than in Russia itself, and so better suited the primitive, barbaric content of 'The Rite'. The bassoon melody as it appears in Stravinsky is played rubato with pauses breaking the flow of the music. It is also ornamented with grace-notes. Compare this with the source in Juszkiewicz, and the difference immediately becomes clear as the Juszkiewicz version is in regular triple time with four-bar phrases and lacks ornamentation:

Stravinsky claimed that this was the only folk quotation in 'The Rite', but it has become clear from work by such authorities as Richard Taruskin that Juszkiewicz provided source material for other themes as well, e.g. in 'Ritual of Abduction', a frantic melody in 9/8 in constant quavers is a reworking of a duple-time original:

Other features of Stravinsky's melodic writing point to the influence of folk song. In the course of 'The Augurs of Spring', two further themes appear, the first on flute on its first hearing which sounds more obviously folk-derived. As the movement progresses, this theme is broken down and its elements reformed. The other theme opens with repeated notes and then moves up and down by step. Also noteworthy in this connection is the narrow range of this melody, and this is the case with other melodies, e.g. the theme for cor anglais which occurs shortly after the opening. On the other hand, there are examples of more angular writing, especially in the introduction where intervals of 7ths appear in a motif which also involves scotch snaps.

In 'The Rite', Stravinsky seemed to be moving in two directions, at first sight mutually exclusive. The purely nationalist folk element at times gives way to primitivism, most evident in the stamping chords and ostinato running throughout 'The Augurs of Spring', a steady duple-time passage involving asymmetrical stresses. Yet this primitive sound is harmonically sophisticated as it is a bitonal structure composed of Fb major and Ab dominant 7th chords, and throughout this section of the work, a number of strikingly dissonant but innovative harmonic structures appear: piled up 4ths and 5ths (though it should be noted that Ravel's 'Daphnis et Chloé' opens with the building up of a chord composed of 5ths). Other devices include drones and parallel movement, both suggesting folk influences, the parallelism often involving side-shifts of dense chords, e.g. 7ths.

It seems that though Stravinsky picked up from where other Russian composers had taken their national music, he developed it as far as it could be taken, culminating in the strikingly original ballet 'Les Noces' (The Wedding), at which point he took up neo-classicism (e.g. 'Pulcinella'). There are few 'barbaric' moments in his later works, although there are savage gestures faintly reminiscent of 'The Rite' in the much later 'Symphony in Three Movements'.

Examiner's points

This essay covers many of the main points, sometimes in passing, especially in the case of rhythm. Extensive background knowledge is evident, both regarding nationalism in the 19th century and the sources of folk-song used in *The Rite*. Musical examples are well used, and there is a clear understanding of the historical significance of this work. This essay would most probably be awarded a mark in the Level 5 band.

Glossary

Acciaccatura. A very short ornamental note played before a principal melodic note, written or printed as ♪

Additive rhythm. Where a bar has beats of unequal length, or where unequal short rhythmic sets are grouped together to form a longer rhythmic pattern.

Aeolian mode. A scale that uses the following pattern of tones (T) and semitones (s): T–s–T–T–s–T–T. When starting on A, it consists of all the white notes within one octave on a keyboard.

Alap. The opening section of a piece of Indian classical music, usually with melodic improvisation and free rhythm, developing into a **rāg**.

Alberti bass. A particular type of broken chord pattern often found in classical keyboard music with three pitches heard in the order low-high-middle-high, e.g. C–G–E–G.

Aleatoric. Music that contains an element of chance or choice on the part of the performer, meaning that its exact course cannot be predicted until it is performed. Music of this kind can also be called 'indeterminate'.

Anacrusis. Note or notes preceding the first beat of a piece or phrase.

Angular. When applied to melody, the presence of wide leaps.

Anthem. A type of church music for choir, often accompanied by organ, and occasionally by larger forces. An anthem usually has English words (often from the Bible).

Antiphony. Performance by different singers/instrumentalists in alternation. Often – but not always – the different groups perform similar material.

Appoggiatura. A non-chord note that sounds on the beat as a dissonance and then resolves by step (up or down) to the main chord note. The dissonant note is not 'prepared' as a suspension is. Although appoggiaturas are normally approached by leap, accented passing notes that are particularly long and/or prominent are often described as appoggiaturas, even though they are approached by step. Sometimes an appoggiatura, especially in the Classical period, is indicated by a note in small type, followed by its resolution printed at normal size.

Arco. A direction to bow notes on a string instrument.

Aria. A song (usually from an **opera**, oratorio or **cantata**) for solo voice, plus accompaniment for orchestra or, sometimes in Baroque times, for smaller forces, even just **continuo**. An aria often provides a character in an opera with the opportunity to reflect at length on their emotional state.

Articulation. The manner in which a series of notes are played with regards to their separation or connection – for example, staccato (separated) or legato (connected).

Atonal. Atonal music avoids keys or modes; that is, no pitch stands out consistently in the way that the tonic does in tonal music.

Augmentation. The lengthening of the rhythmic values of a previously-heard melody (e.g. where ♩ ♫ has become 𝅗𝅥 ♩♩).

Augmented triad. A three-note chord in which the interval between successive notes is a major 3rd; for example, the chord D–F♯–A♯.

Augmented 6th chord. A chromatic chord which in root position spans the interval of an augmented 6th, e.g. A♭–F♯.

Auxiliary note. A type of passing note that moves away and then returns to the main beat note by step, e.g. D–C–D or G–A–G.

Bebop. A style of jazz that developed in the 1940s from swing. More complex and less easy to dance to, it was characterised by **improvisation**, fast tempos, irregular phrase lengths and a greater emphasis on the rhythm section.

Binary form. A structure consisting of two sections, the first of which closes in a related key and the second in the tonic. This structure was frequently used by Baroque composers, e.g. in dance movements.

Bitonal. Music that uses two different keys simultaneously.

Broken chord. The performing of the notes of a chord one after another instead of simultaneously.

Cadence. A pair of chords signifying the end of a phrase in tonal music. Cadences are of several types, of which perfect and imperfect are by far the most common. *See also* **Imperfect cadence**, **Interrupted cadence**, **Perfect cadence**, **Plagal cadence** and **Phrygian cadence**.

Cadential 6-4. Chord Ic, preceding chord V or V⁷ in a perfect or imperfect cadence.

Canon. A strict form of **imitation**, in which each successive part repeats exactly the music of the first part.

Cantata. Most commonly a work for voice(s) and instruments in several movements, with **aria**(s), **recitative**(s) and chorus(es). A cantata can be sacred or secular.

Chorale. A German hymn of the kind sung in the Lutheran (Protestant) church in the time of J. S. Bach. The word 'chorale' can refer to the words only, to the associated melody only, or to the whole hymn. Chorale melodies are largely stepwise (or **conjunct**); their harmonisation has long featured in advanced music courses.

Chordal. A form of homophony in which all the parts move together in the same or very similar rhythm. The term **homorhythmic** (literally 'same rhythm') is sometimes used instead.

Chromatic. A chromatic note is one that does not belong to the scale of the key currently in use. For example, in D major the notes G♯ and C♮ are chromatic.

Circle of 5ths. A harmonic progression in which the roots of the chords move by descending 5ths (and/or ascending 4ths), e.g. B–E–A–D–G–C etc.

Coda. A concluding section of a movement.

Compound time. A metre in which the main beat is subdivided into three equal portions, as opposed to two equal portions in simple time.

Concerto. Most commonly, a work for a soloist with orchestra. In many concertos the solo instrument is a piano or violin. Occasionally there may be two soloists (a double concerto) or even three (a triple concerto). (In the 17th century the term was used more widely, and was applied originally to a work in which voices and instruments, with more or less independent parts, collaborated in a manner that was new at the time.) *See also* **Concerto grosso**.

Concerto grosso. A type of concerto, most common in the late Baroque period, in which three (or occasionally more) soloists, known as the 'concertino', are contrasted with the sound of a larger group of mainly string instruments, known as the 'ripieno'.

Conjunct. Melodic movement by step rather than by leap. Opposite of **disjunct**.

Con sordino. Played with a mute, thereby altering the timbre of the instrument (string and brass instruments).

Continuo. Short for 'basso continuo', the continuo instruments form the accompaniment in Baroque music. It may include instruments such as the harpsichord (capable of playing full harmony) and a cello or bassoon reinforcing the bass line.

Contrapuntal. Adjective to describe music that uses **counterpoint**.

Counterpoint. Counterpoint involves two or more melodic lines (usually rhythmically contrasted), each significant in itself, which are played or sung together at the same time. The term polyphonic is often used as a synonym for contrapuntal.

Countersubject. In a fugue, the melodic material that is heard in counterpoint with the answer.

Course. Two or more adjacent strings on an instrument that are intended to be played as a single string.

Cross rhythm. The use of two or more very different rhythms simultaneously in different parts. One rhythm may imply one metre (or time signature), while another implies a different one.

Cue. This term refers to a particular portion of music intended for inclusion at a specific point of a film.

Development. The central part of a **sonata form** movement between the **exposition** and the recapitulation, containing a working-out of ideas already heard in the exposition.

Dialogue. When two or more instruments or voices have a musical 'conversation', with the individual parts responding to one another.

Diatonic. Using notes that belong to the current key. A diatonic note is one that belongs to the scale of the key currently in use. For example, in D major the notes D, E and F♯ are diatonic.

Diminished 7th chord. A four-note chord made up of superimposed minor 3rds.

Diminished interval. An interval that is one semitone narrower than a minor or perfect interval. A diminished 4th (e.g. G♯–C) is one semitone narrower than a perfect 4th (G–C); a diminished 6th (e.g. B–G♭) is one semitone narrower than a minor 6th (B–G).

Diminution. The shortening of the rhythmic values of a previously-heard melody (e.g. where ♩ ♪♪ has become ♩ ♫).

Disjunct. Melodic movement by leap rather than by step. Opposite of **conjunct**.

Dissonance. Strictly speaking, any note not belonging to a triad in root position or first inversion (even the 4th above the bass in a second inversion counts as dissonant). Some dissonances, particularly suspensions and appoggiaturas, add tension, which in early music had to be 'resolved'; others, notably passing and auxiliary notes, provide rhythmic and melodic decoration.

Dominant 7th chord. A four-note chord built on the dominant (fifth) note of the scale. It includes the dominant triad plus a minor 7th above the root.

Dorian mode. A scale that uses the following pattern of tones (T) and semitones (s): T–s–T–T–T–s–T. When starting on D, it consists of all the white notes within one octave on a keyboard.

Double-stopping. The playing of two notes simultaneously on adjacent strings of a string instrument. The term is sometimes used loosely to cover three- and four-note multiple stopping. *See also* **Triple-stopping**.

Drone. A sustained note (or notes frequently forming an interval of a 5th) held in one part while other parts play or sing melodies against it.

Dynamics. How loudly or softly the music is played; the volume of the music. Indicated by dynamic markings such as *piano* (quiet) and *crescendo* (gradually get louder).

Enlightenment. This term refers to a movement in the 18th century characterised by the exercise of reason and a critical reaction to established forms of religion. Leading enlightenment figures in France included Voltaire and Diderot, and in the United Kingdom, the Scottish philosopher David Hume.

Exposition. The first section of a **sonata form** movement, typically including the first subject in the tonic and the second subject in a related key.

Fall off. In jazz, a short downward slide ending in silence.

False relation. The occurrence of the ordinary and chromatically altered versions of the same note (such as F♮ and F♯) in two different parts at the same time, or in close proximity.

Figured bass. A figured bass is an instrumental bass part with 'figures' or 'figuring' (chiefly numerals and sharp, flat and natural signs) designed to show a continuo keyboard or lute player what type of chord to play.

First inversion. *See* **Inversion**.

Flutter-tonguing. A technique on wind instruments of rolling an 'r' while blowing, that creates a trill-like sound, more common in 20th century music.

Fragmentation. The splitting up of melodic lines into shorter components, which are then treated in isolation.

Fugal. *See* **Fugue**.

Fugato. A passage in **fugal** style which forms part of a larger piece of music.

Fugue. A type of piece in which a main theme called a 'subject' is treated in imitation by all the parts. 'Episodes' are the contrasting sections which depart from this pattern.

Functional harmony. A type of harmony that gravitates to the tonic through use of a hierarchy of chords, the dominant being second only to the tonic, and cadences.

Gamelan. An ensemble from Indonesia (usually Bali or Java) consisting largely of tuned percussion.

Glissando. A slide from one pitch to another.

Ground bass. Also called a ground. A bass **ostinato** or constantly repeating bass pattern, above which a melody unfolds. A popular genre of the early- and mid-Baroque period.

Half-valving. The partial opening of a valve on a brass instrument to result in a weak tone and unfocused pitch. The technique is particularly used in jazz.

Harmonics. A technique of lightly touching the string (e.g. on a violin) to produce a high, flute-like sound.

Hemiola. The articulation of two units of triple time (strong–weak–weak, strong–weak–weak) as three units of duple time (strong–weak, strong–weak, strong–weak).

Heterophony. A type of texture in which a melody is performed simultaneously with one or more rhythmically and/or melodically varied versions of itself.

Homophony. A texture in which one part has a melody and the other parts accompany, in contrast to contrapuntal writing, where each part has independent melodic and rhythmic interest.

Homorhythm. *See* **Chordal**.

Idée fixe. A term associated originally with Berlioz's music, signifying a recurring musical **motif**.

Imitation. Where a melodic idea in one part is immediately repeated in another part (exactly or inexactly), at the same or a different pitch, while the first part continues. Described with the adjective imitative.

Imperfect cadence. An open-ended cadence in which the dominant chord (V) is preceded by any other suitable chord, often I, ii or IV.

Impressionism. A compositional movement that began in France in the late 19th century and continued into the 20th, and was in some respects similar to the art movement of the same name. Important characteristics of Impressionist music include heightened attention to timbre, colour and atmosphere, non-functional harmony and tonality and fluid metre.

Improvisation. Characteristic of jazz, the spontaneous creation of new music, often based on existing musical material (such as a chord pattern).

Incidental music. Music usually written for stage, film or television, which establishes an appropriate atmosphere for the action it accompanies.

Interrupted cadence. A cadence most frequently consisting of chords V–VI, designed to defeat expectations by avoiding chord I.

Inversion (harmonic). When a chord has a note other than the root in the lowest part, it is an inversion. In a first-inversion chord the 3rd of the chord is in the lowest part, and in a second-inversion chord the 5th. For example, a triad of F major in first inversion is A–C–F, and in second inversion is C–F–A. *See also* **Root position**.

Inversion (melodic). When a melody line is heard upside down, e.g. pitches C–E–D are presented as C–A–B.

Inverted pedal. A pedal note which is held in a higher part of the texture, rather than in the bass.

Ionian mode. A scale that uses the following pattern of tones (T) and semitones (s): T–T–s–T–T–T–s. When starting on C, it consists of all the white notes within one octave on a keyboard.

Jhala. In Indian classical music, the fast-paced conclusion of a **rāg**.

Leading note. The seventh degree of a major or minor scale, usually with a strong tendency to rise to the tonic.

Leitmotif. A theme that is associated with a character, situation, mood, object or idea, especially in the operas of Richard Wagner and dramatic works/film music of later composers.

Libretto. The script or words for a dramatic work that is set to music (e.g. an **opera**, musical or oratorio).

Lydian mode. A scale that uses the following pattern of tones (T) and semitones (s): T–T–T–s–T–T–s. When starting on F, it consists of all the white notes within one octave on a keyboard. When the fourth is raised in a major scale, this is sometimes termed a Lydian inflection.

Melismatic. The setting of several notes to one syllable.

Melody-dominated homophony. A melody and accompaniment texture in which the accompaniment is not strictly chordal.

Metre. The metre refers to the pulse of the music and is indicated by the time signature.

Middle 8. The central, contrasting section of a song, also called the bridge, or B section in AABA song form. Often, but not always, eight bars long.

Miniature. A short instrumental piece that depicts a scene or represents a mood.

Minimalism. A 20th- and 21st-century often deliberately simple style of composing based on repetitions of short melodic and rhythmic patterns. It was developed by American composers such as Steve Reich, Philip Glass and Terry Riley.

Mixolydian. One of the modes; this mode is the same as a major scale, except for its lowered seventh note, i.e. the scale running from G to G on the white notes of the piano.

Modal. A term often used to refer to music based on a mode rather than on major and minor keys.

Modulation. A change of key, or the process of changing key.

Monody. A term used in connection with early Baroque music in particular, referring to a solo vocal line accompanied by continuo instruments only.

Monophony. Music consisting only of a single melodic line. Also described with the adjective 'monophonic'.

Motet. A type of church music for choir, sometimes accompanied by organ, and occasionally by larger forces. A motet often has Latin words (commonly from the Bible), and is particularly but not exclusively associated with Roman Catholic services. Motets were often composed for specific occasions, unlike the Ordinary of the Mass.

Motif. A short but distinctive musical idea that is developed in various ways in order to create a longer passage of music. The adjective is 'motivic'.

Moto perpetuo. A piece or part of a piece built on constant rapid movement.

Neapolitan 6th chord. A chromatic chord (often in a minor key) consisting of the first inversion of the major chord formed on the flattened supertonic, i.e. the second degree of the scale (in D minor, for example, the Neapolitan 6th has the notes G–B♭–E♭).

Obbligato. A prominent (and essential – 'obligatory') instrumental part in Baroque music, often in an aria, in addition to the vocal part and **continuo**.

Opera. A large-scale dramatic work for singers and instrumentalists in which the whole text, or most of it, is sung.

Ornamentation. Addition of melodic decoration, often through the use of conventional forms such as trills and mordents.

Ostinato. A repeating melodic, harmonic or rhythmic motif, heard continuously throughout part or the whole of a piece.

Parallelism. Also known as parallel harmony, this is the parallel movement of two or more melodic lines or chords.

Passing note. A non-harmony note approached and quitted by step in the same direction, often filling in a melodic gap of a 3rd (e.g. A between G and B, where both G and B are harmony notes).

Pedal (note). A sustained or repeated note, usually in a low register, over which changing harmonies occur. A pedal on the fifth note of the scale (a dominant pedal) tends to create a sense of expectation in advance of a perfect cadence; a pedal on the keynote (a tonic pedal) can create a feeling of repose.

Pentatonic. A scale made up of five notes, most frequently the first, second, third, fifth and sixth degrees of a major scale (for example, C pentatonic is C–D–E–G–A).

Perfect cadence. A cadence consisting of the dominant chord (V or V⁷) followed by the tonic (I).

Periodic phrasing. In Classical-period music particularly, where phrases of regular length are heard in balanced structures. The expression 'antecedent and consequent' is sometimes applied to these phrases.

Phrygian cadence. A type of imperfect cadence, in which the dominant chord (V) is preceded by the first inversion of the subdominant (IVb). It is used chiefly in minor keys, and particularly in Baroque music.

Pitch bend. In jazz, a microtonal variation in pitch.

Pizzicato (often abbreviated to **pizz.**). A direction to pluck, instead of bow, string(s) on a violin, viola, cello or double bass. Cancelled by the direction '**arco**' – with the bow.

Plagal cadence. A cadence consisting of the subdominant chord followed by the tonic (IV–I).

Pointillism. Originally referring to a painting technique, in which small dots of colour are carefully placed to create a larger image, this refers to a musical effect in which different notes are played or sung in isolation from each other, rather than as part of a musical line, thereby sketching out a larger musical form.

Polyphony. Sometimes used as an alternative term for **counterpoint**, especially in relation to Renaissance music.

Polyrhythm. The use of more than one rhythm at the same time, often implying the presence of different metres.

Post-modernism. A style of composition that deliberately contrasts itself with modernist concepts, and the highly intellectual approach (typified by serialism) associated with them. Post-modernism tries to avoid categorising music rigidly, and often incorporates fragments of works and references to other cultures in a more approachable style.

Programmatic. Music with a stimulus that comes from outside the music itself.

Quartal harmony. Harmony based on the interval of a 4th (e.g. with chords such as A–D–G), rather than on the interval of a 3rd as in triads and 7th chords.

Quarter tone. Half a semitone.

Rāg. A scale pattern or melodic motif used as the basis for melodic improvisation in Indian classical music.

Recapitulation. In **sonata form**, the section which follows the **development**. It is often closely based on the **exposition**, but normally both opens and closes in the tonic key.

Recitative. A piece for solo voice in an **opera**, **cantata** or oratorio (often before an aria) in which clear projection of words is the main concern. In many recitatives the music is functional rather than of great interest in itself, with the accompaniment often just for **continuo**.

Retrograde. The pitches of a previously heard melody or rhythm presented in reverse order.

Riff. In popular music styles, a short repeating phrase.

Ritornello form. A structure used in Baroque music in which an opening instrumental section (called the ritornello) introduces the main musical ideas. This returns, often in shortened versions and in related keys, between passages for one or more soloists. The complete ritornello (or a substantial part of it) returns in the tonic key at the end.

Rondo. A form in which the main theme (or subject) returns periodically in the tonic key. Simple rondo takes the form A–B–A–C–A etc., while Sonata rondo involves recapitulation of a second subject as well as the first: A–B(related key)–A–C(development)–A–B(tonic)–A. This form came to be used frequently in finales.

Root position. A chord that has the root in the lowest sounding part.

Rounded binary form. A variation of simple **binary form** (AB), in which a thematic reference to the beginning of the moment is made at the end of the B section.

Rubato. The variation of pulse by subtle lengthening and shortening of notes, so producing a free rhythmic feel.

Saltarello. A lively dance in $\frac{6}{8}$ which originated from Naples in the 13th century.

Scherzo. A fast movement which eventually replaced the minuet of the Classical era.

Scotch snap. A two-note pattern in dotted rhythm (short-long), producing a distinctive effect.

Secondary dominant. A passing or temporary dominant hinting at a different key, e.g. in C major, an E major chord acting as dominant to a tonic of A minor.

Secondary 7th. A 7th chord built on a degree of the scale other than the dominant.

Second inversion. *See* **Inversion**.

Sequence. Immediate repetition of a melodic or harmonic idea at a different pitch.

Siciliano. A type of movement found particularly in 17th- and 18th-century music characterised by a slow $\frac{6}{8}$ or $\frac{12}{8}$ time signature. It often included dotted rhythms.

Simple time. A metre in which the main beat is sub-divided into two equal portions. Opposite of **compound time**.

Singspiel. A type of German language opera with spoken dialogue in place of the recitative that separates the arias, ensemble numbers and choruses in other types of opera

Sonata. An instrumental work, commonly in three or four movements. From the late Baroque period onwards, sonatas are usually for solo keyboard or for single melody instrument and keyboard. 'Trio sonatas' (middle to late Baroque) are normally for two violins and continuo.

Sonata form. Typical first movement form of the Classical and Romantic periods. In three sections – **exposition**, **development**, **recapitulation** – often based on two groups of melodic material in two contrasting keys (first subject, second subject).

Stretto. The overlapping of imitative entries more closely than had previously occurred, used especially in connection with **fugal** writing.

Strophic form. A structure found mainly in simple songs in which the same music is used for each of several verses. The form can be expressed as AAA... etc.

Substitution chord. A chord that is substituted for another chord for the sake of variety. In particular the term is used in jazz.

Sul ponticello. On a stringed instrument, bowed near the bridge, producing a thin, harsh sound quality.

Suspension. A suspension occurs at a change of chord, when one part hangs on to (or repeats) a note from the old chord, creating a clash, after which the delayed part resolves by step (usually down) to a note of the new chord.

Swung rhythm. In jazz and other popular music, a certain freedom in performance whereby rhythms that might in other contexts be played 'straight' as equal notes are performed with the first of each pair longer than the second, often giving a kind of triplet effect.

Syllabic. The setting of one note to one syllable.

Symphony. A work for orchestra with several (usually three or four) movements in different tempi – in effect a sonata for orchestra rather than for one or a few instruments.

Syncopation. The shifting of stress from a strong to a weak beat.

Ternary form. A musical structure of three sections in which the outer sections are similar and the central one contrasting (ABA).

Terraced dynamics. Bold, abrupt contrasts between loud and soft, with no crescendo or diminuendo marks. Mid-volume dynamics, such as *mp* and *mf*, are avoided

Tertiary progression. When roots of chords or key areas proceed by 3rds.

Tessitura. A specific part of a singer's or instrument's range. For example a 'high tessitura' indicates a high part of the range.

Texture. The relationship between the various simultaneous lines in a passage of music, dependent on such features as the number and function of the parts and the spacing between them.

Through-composed. Applied to music in which the composer avoids repetition of previous material, i.e. fresh material for different phrases in a vocal work.

Tierce de Picardie. A major 3rd in the final tonic chord of a passage in a minor key.

Timbre. The element of music concerned with the actual sound quality, or tone colour, of the music.

Tonality. Music is described as being tonal when one note is of central importance, other notes being subordinate. The note of central importance is termed the tonic when major and minor keys and scales are used. In 18th-and 19th-century music tonality is established and maintained by functional harmony, but tonality can be based instead on other types of scales, notably modes.

Transition. A linking passage.

Tremolo. A rapid and continuous repetition of a single note or two alternating notes.

Trill. An ornament in which two adjacent notes rapidly and repeatedly alternate (the note bearing the trill sign and the one above it). The symbol for trill is *tr*.

Tripartite form. A three-part form, typically A–B–C (as in 16th and 17th century pavane and galliard dance movements), as distinct from ternary form (A–B–A) movements.

Triple-stopping. The playing of three notes simultaneously (or as near simultaneously as possible) on adjacent strings of a string instrument. *See also* **Double-stopping**.

Triplet. A group of three equal notes played in the time normally taken by two notes of the same type.

Tritone. An interval that is equivalent to three tones (an augmented 4th or dimished 5th).

Turn. A four-note ornament that 'turns' around the main note. It starts on the note above, drops to the main note, drops to the note below and then returns to the main note. Indicated by the symbol ∾.

Twelve-bar blues. A standard chord sequence used in the blues and other popular music, which is based on the tonic (I), subdominant (IV) and dominant (V) chords of a key. Its most common form is I–I–I–I, IV–IV–I–I, V–IV–I–I.

Una corda. The soft pedal on a piano, so that only one string plays rather than three.

Unison. Simultaneous performance of the same note or melody by two or more players or singers.

Walking bass. A bass part that persistently uses the same note length.

Whole-tone scale. A scale in which the interval between every successive note is a whole tone.

Acknowledgements:

The Duchess
Music by Rachel Portman.
© Copyright 2008 Berkeley Music
Publishing Co., Bucks Music Group Ltd.
All Rights Reserved.
International Copyright Secured.

Batman Returns
Music by Daniel Elfman.
© Copyright 1992 Warner-Barham Music
LLC. Universal/MCA Music Limited.
All Rights Reserved.
International Copyright Secured.

Psycho
Music by Bernard Herrmann.
© Copyright 1960 Sony/ATV Melody.
Famous Music Corporation.
All Rights Reserved.
International Copyright Secured.

Eleanor Rigby
Words and music by John Lennon and
Paul McCartney. © Copyright 1966
Sony/ATV Music Publishing.
All Rights Reserved.
International Copyright Secured.

Here, There and Everywhere
Words and music by John Lennon and
Paul McCartney.
© Copyright 1966 Sony/ATV Tunes
LLCD/B/A. Sony/ATV Music Publishing.
All Rights Reserved.
International Copyright Secured.

I Want to Tell You
Words and music by George Harrison.
© Copyright 1966 Northern Songs Ltd.
Sony/ATV Music Publishing.
All Rights Reserved.
International Copyright Secured.

Burn
Words by Salim Merchant, music by
Anoushka Shankar, Salim Merchant,
Utkarsha Kale and Gaurav Raina.
© Copyright 2007 Anourag Music
Publishing/Merchant Music Publishing
(UK)/Mighty Junn Music/GR Music
Publishing. Bucks Music Group Limited/
Chester Music Limited.
All Rights Reserved.
International Copyright Secured.

Breathing Under Water
Words and music by Anoushka Shankar,
Utkarsha Kale and Gaurav Raina.
© Copyright 2007 Anourag Music
Publishing/Mighty Junn Music/GR Music
Publishing. Bucks Music Group Limited/
Chester Music Limited.
All Rights Reserved.
International Copyright Secured.

Easy
Words by Norah Jones, music by Norah
Jones, Anoushka Shankar, Utkarsha Kale
and Gaurav Raina. © Copyright 2007
Anourag Music Publishing/Mighty
Junn Music/GR Music Publishing.
Copyright Control/Chester Music Limited/
Bucks Music Group Limited.

The Rite of Spring
Music by Igor Stravinsky.
© Copyright 1913 Hawkes & Son (London)
Limited. All Rights Reserved.
International Copyright Secured.

Blackpool Sixth
FYi Library
01253 394911
fyi@blackpoolsixth.ac.uk